Managing to Manage

Managing to Manage
The essential guide to people management

DEREK TORRINGTON

KoganPage

LONDON   PHILADELPHIA   NEW DELHI

658.3
TOR

54283619

First published in Great Britain and the United States in 2013 by Kogan Page Limited

120 Pentonville Road	1518 Walnut Street, Suite 1100	Ansari Road
London N1 9JN	Philadelphia PA 19102	Daryaganj
United Kingdom	USA	New Delhi 110002
www.koganpage.com		India

© Derek Torrington 2013

The right of Derek Torrington to be identified as the author of this work has been asserted by him in accordance with the Copyright, Designs and Patents Act 1988.

ISBN   978 0 7494 6674 9
E-ISBN   978 0 7494 6675 6

British Library Cataloguing in Publication Data

A CIP record for this book is available from the British Library.

Library of Congress Cataloging-in-Publication Data

Torrington, Derek, 1931-
    Managing to manage : the essential guide to people management / Derek Torrington.
        p. cm.
    Includes index.
    ISBN 978-0-7494-6674-9 – ISBN 978-0-7494-6675-6 (ebook) 1. Management. 2. Personnel management. 3. Interpersonal relations. I. Title.
    HD31.T643 2013
    658.4--dc23
                        2012041084

Typeset by Amnet
Printed and bound in India by Replika Press Pvt Ltd

Contents

Preface

This book is about how to do the management part of your job now, whether you are a novice or an expert. It is not about how to get rich but how to get home from work satisfied that you have done well that day. It is not about being an entrepreneur, but about managing to get things done, and done effectively.

It is fine to be ambitious, to aim for the stars or to set out to change the world, but dreams are rarely fulfilled by guts and idealism alone. Some years ago, the then head of the charity Shelter, the campaign for the homeless, described the problem of finding the right staff – many behaved as if Shelter was not a campaign for the homeless but a home for the campaigners: 'I need people who will stuff envelopes and then stuff some more. I don't want them endlessly drinking coffee and having wonderful debates about inequality.'

This book is mainly for people new to management responsibilities or having difficulty with those they already have, but not exclusively. If you are a powerful chief executive leafing through this book during a flight to Hong Kong to see if it might be of some use to junior staff, just try the little exercise in Chapter 11 when you get back to the office.

I hope you like it. I've really enjoyed writing it!

Introduction

This book introduces managing with people to those of you who have not the time or inclination to study it properly. It is certainly not for HR professionals, but for scientists and engineers, for lawyers and accountants, for nurses and police officers, for technical advisers and school teachers, for social workers, for librarians and actuaries, perhaps even for authors and lecturers. It is for those who spend most of their working lives managing their participation in a managed system, but who do not see managing people as their main job. They have far more important matters to worry about, but cannot avoid such things as occasionally interviewing someone applying for a job or doing a bit of training or joining a team and wondering why every other member of it is such a pain.

In preparing for the job you now do, you have probably spent most of your time studying in disciplines which encourage you to seek logic, precision and clarity. You are now pretty clear about what actions produce what results in professional and technical aspects of your job. In contrast, this book tries to explain how men and women cope with each other at work: a social world which is often unpredictable and frustrating. I will be using material drawn from a range of social sciences, which are typically less precise and less scientific than, for instance, the physical sciences or accountancy or medicine or engineering. Coping with this difference is essential; even the most brilliant people can be ineffective (and exasperated) in their work if they cannot work with other people.

The first part of the book deals with the main aspects of managing to manage with people in an organizational context.

You probably don't like long, wordy stuff that rambles on and you would find a series of bullet points so much easier, but these topics need to be well understood. Bullet points are easy to remember but rarely lead to understanding. So these chapters will average around 3,500+ words, and you do have to work at them.

The second part has a series of much shorter 'How to...' guides, to help you do specific things that are essential features of work in the first part of the book. These are easy enough to explain in a few pages, but that will not be enough to guarantee effectiveness, which will require practice and experience, perhaps with further study. Most aspects of management are straightforward common sense, but they all require hard work and right thinking to be done well.

Some further reading is suggested if you want it. I have avoided the usual management literature preoccupation with being up to date. The reason is that the book is about fundamentals and these have been progressively researched and explained over the past 50 to 100 years, so they no longer interest many management researchers. If the best explanations and suggestions were developed many years ago, then that is what will be included, providing that they are still clearly sound and relevant.

Key concepts are introduced progressively through the book. These are a bit like bullet points, to condense the essence of what is being said, but no shirking! Read the chapter first, noting the key concepts as you go along and pausing to say, 'Ah. Mmm'.

KEY CONCEPT 1

Managing with people is working with *people as well as being in charge. We all have to build effective relationships with colleagues in order to get the most out of our jobs while producing good results. Also, we all have to understand how our particular organization works and how we can use it to produce good results. Personnel or human resource management is different. It is a specialist role in a business to enable everyone else in the business to be good at managing with people.*

The managerial role

Fred is a service engineer, installing, maintaining and repairing washing machines and dishwashers. At the beginning of each shift he has a list of customers and notes of what has to be done. He will work out the route to take around the different addresses, taking account of what needs to be done at each, and will then fine-tune his route before starting out. He is managing his work pattern, translating a list of customers into a programme of work. The *Oxford English Dictionary* defines managing as 'having executive control or authority'. He has control, he decides what to do and then implements, or executes, those decisions, although Fred does not see himself as a manager.

Helen is Head of Science in a secondary school. She has to organize a timetable distribution among a staff of 16 science teachers: who is taking which students for which subjects. She is also responsible for the organization of the curriculum that the students will follow. Helen is not a manager and would be reluctant to be described as one, but the dictionary defines management as 'the process of dealing with or controlling things or people'. This is what Helen has to do and she well knows that it is the people who are the tricky bit. She will spend time and energy winning the agreement of the teachers to her organization of the curriculum, probably modifying it in the light of their comments. She will spend even more time dealing with individual arguments about teaching load and time allocation. Fred has a responsible and difficult job of executive control, but he is the person he is controlling, so he can only argue with himself, at the same time explaining the shortcomings of 'the office' to every householder he visits. Helen has to get most of the work done by other people, although she will also do that work herself. The people dimension is where most of the challenges in management are found.

KEY CONCEPT 2

People will support and make a success of what they have helped to create.

John is personnel manager in a business making electronic components. He manages a staff of eight, including a training officer, a recruitment and training officer and a health and safety officer. His specialist expertise is in employment law and psychological testing, which is used as an adjunct to other methods of determining specific aptitudes and potential in new recruits. He works closely with all three specialist officers as his expertise interlocks with theirs. He is also a member of the senior management team that forms overall company strategy and policy. Here he has to represent and explain all human resource issues and implications for all areas of the business.

KEY CONCEPT 3

Managers need to retain their specialist skills if they are to keep the respect of those with whom they work at all levels.

Tina is a middle manager in the Irish subsidiary of a French company. Her official title is 'Vendor Scheduler' and the main objective of her job is to order and organize shipment and delivery of all materials needed for the timely completion of the scheduled production plan. Components are ordered with specific lead-times, purchased at the optimum prices, and kept within predetermined stock levels. Procedures and supplier contracts are set and negotiated by the central purchasing department in France, mainly with French suppliers but also recently negotiated with Indian and Taiwanese suppliers. Fluency in French and familiarity with French business culture are central to Tina's effectiveness. All meetings, video-conferences, e-mails and most telephone calls are in French and few of Tina's Irish colleagues are sufficiently fluent in the language to be effective in these exchanges.

Tina therefore requires high specialist expertise, as do Fred, Helen and John, but the people management function is more about networking outside the business and meetings with other senior people in the business rather than direct supervision. It also requires constant and varying initiatives, deciding what should be done and working out how to do it. This is called agenda-setting. Fred, Helen and John have a limited range of matters to deal with. Fred's list of customers is predetermined, Helen has most of the factors affecting her job decided by others, inside the school or outside, and John has to work within the strategy and overall policy of the management. Sometimes he will not agree with the decisions of the senior management team but he has to accept them and make them work. All three of them have much of their function given to them by other people or by the system within which they work. Tina has the set procedures within which she has to work set by the parent company and its requirements. However, a large part of her work involves working with people outside the organizational boundary and using a foreign language. She illustrates another facet of the manager's job: developing networks and agendas for action.

KEY CONCEPT 4

Managers have two core tasks: working out agendas for action (what to do) and developing networks of contacts to facilitate implementing those agendas (how to get it done).

All those we have described are managing with people.

> **Fred:** When I get my list I'm on my own. I can set my stall out and do what I'm good at. Then people muck things up. I get a call from Betty in the office to say that Mrs Smith has got to go into her child's school because of an emergency but she should be back by 11, so I have to re-jig my route. I have to install a dishwasher at no. 40, but when I get there the auxiliary piping is wrong and I haven't got one on the van. The chap there goes on like it's my fault.

When the people dimension includes managing *of* as well as managing *with* people it gets much more complex.

> **Helen:** I often have to persuade a teacher to do something they really dislike. They all know their subject and I can't interfere with that. I'm a chemist and I can't disagree with a biologist on how to teach human reproduction, but I can decide which biologist should teach which group of students if there are matters outside subject expertise. Sometimes people need to be challenged to leave a comfortable niche and do something different. The head has a broader view of the staff than I do and individual teachers have more things to do in the school than are my responsibility. The hardest thing of all is when you have a failing teacher. For an easy life you would want that person removed, but I can't do that and I always think, 'there but for the grace of God go I…'. How do you help that person to improve instead of failing?

When managing colleagues who have a level of expertise that is greater in some ways than your own, you lose their respect and constructive cooperation if you do not keep yourself in touch with their specialist area.

John: My immediate colleagues know what to do and get on with it. Sometimes they don't agree with aspects of strategy but they accept it as long as they feel it is properly thought through and trust me to represent their views. They all accept that I am in charge, but I know how important it is for me to maintain their confidence by knowing my stuff. The senior management team also have to have confidence in my specialist expertise; otherwise they will ignore what I say.

Having a management job that has little or no managing of people, but a lot of managing with people, especially with people outside the business, triggers different issues.

Tina: I'm dealing with French people who operate differently from the Irish and Irish people who can't speak French, to say nothing of Indians and Taiwanese! In France there is a cynical phrase about business practice: *Pourquoi le faire simple quand on peut le faire compliqué* or 'Why make things simple when you can make them complicated?' This preference for elaboration is in the language. An accurate translation of a letter in English will usually require 25 per cent more words in French than the original.

So everyone does some managing while they are at work, even if it is managing themselves, but almost always it involves other people and these relationships vary according to the work involved and the degree of mutual dependence between the parties.

Part One
What managing is all about

Chapter One
Being a manager

The role, what you do and how you do it

Managerial work varies greatly according to the nature of the responsibilities. The chief executive of a business has a different job from an office manager in the same company. It is not just carrying more responsibility and having more power; the work involved is quite different. To make sense of this variety we have to find features which all management jobs have in common, despite their diversity. Even managers with apparently identical jobs will still do their jobs in different ways because of their temperament and experience.

Different situations require different management approaches. A team of people dealing with the evacuation of a burning building require a management approach that is totally different from that needed by the team who designed the building in the first place. Those working for, with and around managers always want to figure them out and respond to them as individual human beings. Who are they? What do they really think? Which is the particular demon that drives them?

Most managers are constantly changing from one thing to another and changing, furthermore, from one thing to a very different other. Henry Mintzberg is one of the legends in management research and the studies of management work he carried out in the 1970s remain as precise and relevant today as when they were first published. He found that the chief executives he studied made contact, on average, with 52 people each day. Only 10 per cent of tasks took an hour or more, and more than 50 per cent of tasks took less than nine minutes. This differs sharply from the specialization and extended periods of application to a single task that characterize most non-managerial jobs.

The mobile phone, the laptop and the smartphone have made little change in the current pattern, although they have increased the intensity of the managerial day. Most management research is Anglo-American, and this degree of fragmentation is not necessarily found in other cultures. Japanese chief executives have a much less fragmented pattern, partly because hurried contacts are felt to be impolite in these societies, and partly because they tend to have fewer and longer meetings. But it is interesting to speculate what the relative impact might be on effectiveness of having a fragmented or a non-fragmented day. Fragmentation may lead to dealing with matters only superficially.

Managers spend much of their time, between 50 and 80 per cent, in conversation with others. A typical manager in any position spends a little over 10 per cent of their time with superiors, while the remainder of contact time is split fairly evenly between time with subordinates and time with others. Furthermore, they mainly prefer spoken rather than written material and current information and live action rather than considered reports.

This sort of evidence suggests that managers are not in fact devoting their time to planning, decision making and the other types of reflective activity which some textbooks suggest. If, however, we take account of what is being said in all these face-to-face encounters and telephone conversations, often decisions are being taken and plans being laid, although the independent observer may regard the process as lacking system and thoroughness. Similarly, the business lunch or pie and a pint in the pub has considerable potential in information exchanged, discussion and agreement on actions to follow, even though some may consider them a wasteful and self-indulgent method for managers to use to conduct their affairs.

KEY CONCEPT 5

Typically managers spend well over half of their working day in conversation and constantly switching between topics.

If managers spend so much of their time in conversation with a variety of people and they are frequently interrupted, why do they work in this way? There are three distinct strands in the work that managers do: specialist, administrative and managerial. The specialist work of a manager is that work done not because of being a manager, but almost in spite of that fact: work concerned with the main task of the business, section or department, which is probably the work of at least some subordinates as well. It is the head teacher teaching children in the classroom, the chief designer working at a drawing board, the director of research conducting an experiment, the nurse manager discussing infection control, or the garage proprietor tuning the engine on a customer's car.

Specialist work involves the manager using the skills and knowledge acquired through qualifications, training and experience. Managers abandon these skills at their peril, as they can then lose touch with the main task of the department or business, although the management development process in many British businesses appears to encourage managers to let their technical skills atrophy.

Administrative work is concerned with organizational maintenance, while managerial work is taking initiatives, and we can best understand the difference by considering them together. The first is carrying out official, often regular, duties authorized by others, such as the organizational superior or a committee; the other is conducting and controlling organizational affairs with the freedom to create precedents. This brings change, but the change must be improvement. One aspect of the managerial/administrative distinction is intuitively described by many managers when they talk about the scope that a person has to make mistakes or exercise discretion. The greater the discretion, the greater the managerial content of the job and the more one is setting rather than following precedents. It is the greater range of discretion, and especially the greater length of time that will elapse before the effect of mistakes is known, that is one of the distinctive characteristics of management work.

This administrative/managerial distinction can also be expressed in terms of novelty and comfort. Like many human activities, managerial work is active, extrovert and novelty seeking, concerned with initiating and taking risks by setting precedents. Administrative work is a quieter activity, introvert and providing the comfort of familiarity and dealing with what is known. It keeps the system going by maintaining things in working order. A number of psychologists have offered the opinion that the novelty/comfort balance in human beings is always in a state of change, according to the situation in which they find themselves. The behaviour of those facing bereavement is often characterized by actions that are so prosaic as to seem bizarre, like needing to go to the hairdresser or to go shopping, and deciding to decorate the back bedroom or work on the car. This is not callousness but seeking the comfort of the familiar at a time when the crisis is too great to bear.

When managers are faced with too many difficult problems and are uncertain about what to do, they may take great comfort in filling in timesheets, record cards or other routine administrative tasks. The executive briefcase is partly a badge of office ('I am important') but also contains a supply of administrative comforters to go with the indigestion tablets. The first-class compartments of intercity trains are full of managers travelling to meetings and passing the time by 'catching up on their reading' or 'checking through the figures'. On the other hand, when the routine paperwork becomes too oppressive a manager may seek some stimulus to get the adrenalin flowing: they go looking for novelty or excitement.

sSAMp

Over a period of 20 years Jane Weightman and I carried out a range of studies on managerial work, using the study method of close observation over an extended period. The manager subjects just get on with their jobs while the researcher sits, like a fly on the wall, and records every time there is a change of activity. Managers being observed initially find it very puzzling, and sometimes disconcerting, especially if they do not have anything to do! Once that initial uneasiness has been overcome, they forget about the researcher, who is classifying every change of activity by the time it has taken place and the nature of the work involved. The classification uses the shorthand of sSAMp, which uses the following definitions:

'**social**' is the classification for all those everyday social interchanges that take place among people at work, like discussing the TV programme we saw last night and talking about the weather.

'**Specialist, Administrative or Managerial**' classifies activities which fall into one of the categories described above.

'**personal**' is used to describe those personal matters that have to be dealt with while at work, ranging from going to the loo to phoning home to sort out child care, making a doctor's appointment, or 'popping out' to buy a forgotten birthday card.

s and p are deliberately put in lower-case letters as they are less interesting in understanding what managers do than are the S, A and M.

The data in the studies show a considerable range in the time distribution for different managers who were observed, each over a period of several days (Table 1.1). This should not be construed as suggesting that the mean figures are the best way: more significant is the range. Two of the people observed were divisional HR managers in different divisions of the same manufacturing company. The job descriptions were identical, as were the salaries, numbers of office staff, company car entitlement and size of division. Theoretically the jobs and job demands were the same, but the time spent was markedly different (Table 1.2). The range of figures shows how widely individual managers differ from each other, whereas the averages inevitably tend towards an even distribution.

TABLE 1.1   Time distribution for different managers

Classification	Range (%)	Mean (%)
Social and personal	2–50	6
Specialist	0–78	27
Administrative	2–7	29
Managerial	4–86	38

TABLE 1.2   Time distribution for two divisional HR managers

Classification	Job A (%)	Job B (%)
Social and personal	13.5	13.0
Specialist	1.8	26.0
Administrative	56.7	12.4
Managerial	28.0	48.6

The conclusion from these observations is that many managers are uncertain about how to go about their managerial work, because there is no single model to follow, and this leads to the result that they typically do more administrative work than is appropriate simply because it is identifiable and comforting. If there is a set of expense claims to authorize, there is no doubt about (a) what you have to do and (b) when you have done it. This sometimes means that the managerial work does not get done. It is harder to identify, harder to know what to do, and harder still to know whether or not you have done it.

This is not a case for more staff or clerical assistance, as all managers have to do administrative work. The danger is that some allow, or want, administrative work to dominate and to become the purpose of the job itself.

A further conclusion, based on a more general assessment of the demeanour and comments of the managers observed, is that managers need to keep up with specialist work and involvement in order to stay in touch with the people in the organization or section. Managers have to have a very high level indeed of managerial effectiveness and administrative competence if they are to be able to command the respect of their colleagues and subordinates without remaining technically up to date.

KEY CONCEPT 6

The central elements of the work that managers do can be classified as specialist, administrative or managerial. The balance between these three varies between different jobs and even between people with jobs that are notionally identical. Each manager needs to consider very carefully the balance between the three that will lead to effective performance and job satisfaction.

Finding the right balance for effectiveness at the job and personal satisfaction with the work usually means that managers need to reduce the time and effort they spend on administrative activities by delegating them, not doing them at all and reviewing the nature of the administration. The worst crime is to create administrative work for other people to do that is for your own interest rather than being really necessary to get things done. The time saved from this should normally be spent on really coming to terms with your managerial work. This will mean being in touch with the specialist section, so may involve more specialist work. It often also requires negotiating with your own boss to get more managerial work delegated. The boss probably thought you were not interested. The balance to be found depends on the individual personality and on the circumstances of the job. This theme is taken further in Chapter 11.

All managers have two activities in common: setting agendas for action and setting up networks to implement those agendas (Key Concept 4). What do you aim to achieve and who are the people with whom you have to engage to get it done? A moment's thought may lead you to say that that is obvious, and I never say that the job of management is difficult to understand, but often the blindingly obvious is not taken on board until someone points it out.

The word *agenda* describes a list of items to be dealt with, so that it becomes a way of putting into practice the whole range of decisions that are made, such as policy, plans, strategies and agreements. Each of those is an occasional, cerebral act. Setting agendas is the constant activity of managers as plans and ideas are put into operation. 'Increase sales turnover by 25 per cent over the next 12 months' is a wonderfully general statement of an objective, but the manager responsible will try to make that happen by setting up a series of agendas or programmes to bring about the desired result. Some brainstorming and hard-headed analysis may produce an agreement 'to improve our exposure in Eastern Europe', but that will be no more than a general declaration of intent until a manager puts together an agenda of what to do, what to do first, what to check, whom to deploy, whom to ask, when to aim for as a completion date, and so on. The business may have a corporate plan, but the individual managers responsible for achieving the results of the plan will each have a series of agendas, evolving, developing and extending, as the plan becomes a reality.

These frameworks for action are created by a process of thinking out possibilities, constant questioning and aggressively gathering information, with the questioning aided by a shrewd knowledge of the business. Choices are made both analytically and intuitively as careful calculation is combined with skilled guessing to move into action. The agendas are seldom written, although many lists are jotted down on the backs of envelopes, and may be either vague or specific, according to the subject matter. The versatility of modern smartphones encourages some managers to write and constantly update their agendas on this device. This can have the advantage that the owners appear to regard the smartphone as an appendage directly connected to their central nervous system that needs to be consulted at every available opportunity, whereas the back of the envelope can get forgotten or lost.

Agenda-setting is one way in which managers impose their will on the situation around them; the other is by setting up and maintaining networks through which the agendas are implemented. These are different from the formal structure, although no substitute for it. Networks are the means of political activity by managers. The individual manager identifies a large number of people, both inside the organization and outside, who will help in implementing agendas, as well as being sources of information to go into agendas. The popular picture of the manager constantly making telephone calls is an expression of the network process of 'having a word with' contacts: the people who help to get things done by speeding something up, providing information, jumping a queue, endorsing a proposal in committee, checking data, arranging for the manager to meet someone and, of course, doing jobs. Networks are peopled partly by subordinates, but by a large variety of others, including those who have some respect for the manager, those who are dependent on or under obligation to the manager. No manager can operate by remote control, simply making decisions and issuing instructions; they have to manage with and through people. The people may not initially understand, they may have better ideas, they may have to be persuaded. Position in the hierarchy is crucial to having a good network, but so is expertise and social skilfulness. Methods used to set up networks include using disarming candour, doing small favours for others, being a 'nice guy', building a team of willing subordinates and generally shaping the relationships among the people in the network. In recent years networking has received much greater emphasis as part of the general process in organizations of de-layering and downsizing. Managers become more dependent on outside sources, so their pocket personal organizer or mobile phone has an ever-increasing list of names, phone numbers and notes about usefulness. The internet increases the networking potential enormously.

Agenda-setting emphasizes analysis, imagination and planning; networking emphasizes social skill and political judgement. All managers do both, but the most effective are those with equal skill in both areas. Chapter 12 deals with networking more fully.

The management job

I have been describing various ways of classifying managerial work as a means of understanding the range and variety of the managerial role. I have avoided a definition of management or of manager because any definition tends to exclude as many jobs as it includes. The essence of management appears in so many different jobs. Many scientists and engineers do not see themselves as managers at all, even though much of what they do would be included in any categorization of managerial work.

Most people at work, and certainly most qualified people, have aspects of management in their role. We have seen so far that managers, whether with that title or not, have a subtle and varied job, although the core behaviours of making agendas and operating networks are so simple that the detractor is inclined to say that the manager's job has been inflated out of all proportion and that any subtlety and complexity are around the job rather than in what managers actually do.

Most other jobs have an immediate inbuilt purpose and logic: there is an obvious task to be carried through – a demand placed on the job holder. The schoolteacher faces the classroom of children waiting to be occupied, the plumber has a burst pipe to repair, the chef has customers waiting for food to be cooked, and the laboratory assistant has a piece of equipment to set up. The job is clear in its logic, which is to translate a demand from the organizational system into activities or tasks to be undertaken by the job holder *and there is a clear result*. Managers have some aspects of their jobs that are like this: the in-tray full of papers, the constant flow of e-mail to be dealt with, the outgoing letters to sign, the telephone to be answered. These are responses, mainly administrative, to demands from the system of the organization. An activity of a manager is to read letters that arrive in much the same way as the activity of a postman is to deliver the letters in the first place. How the manager responds to the letter will be one aspect of how management work differs from other work, as it is likely to involve some aspects of problem solving and decision making with features of coordination and command. It is still, however, reacting to a situation and responding to the initiatives of others. Managers studied in research projects usually describe these activities – mail, paperwork, answering the telephone, dealing with enquiries – as time-consuming and unsatisfying. They prefer those activities where they impose their own logic on a task rather than the task having its own logic which is imposed on the manager. They prefer making things happen or being proactive instead of reactive.

FURTHER READING

The seminal work on what managers do is Mintzberg, H (1973) *The Nature of Managerial Work*, Harper & Row, London, followed by Mintzberg, H (1975) The manager's job: folklore and fact, *Harvard Business Review*, July/August, pp 49–61. A book to read as a follow-up to Mintzberg is Kotter, J (1982) *The General Managers*, Free Press, New York, and *What Leaders Really Do* (1999). Kotter is also known for his work on power, *Power and Influence* (1985) also published by Free Press, New York.

Jeffrey Pfeffer has specialized in studying power, principally in Pfeffer, J (1981) *Power in Organizations*, Pitman, Marshfield, MA, but steadily developing his ideas until *Power: Why some people have it and others don't*, Harper Collins, New York, 2010.

Anyone interested in reading more about sSAMp could look up Torrington, DP and Weightman, JB (1982) Technical atrophy in middle management, *Journal of General Management*, 7 (3), Spring, pp 5–17 or Torrington, DP and Weightman, JB (1987) Middle management work, *Journal of General Management*, 13 (2), Winter, pp 74–89. When the work was first published we used the term 'technical' instead of 'specialist', but this led many people to assume it was only about engineers, so we now find 'specialist' preferable, although sSAMp does not trip as easily off the tongue as sTAMp.

Chapter Two
Being part of
a business

You are not alone

KEY CONCEPT 7

The manager is not alone. Everybody at work has some degree of independence, but they are inescapably part of something. You are actually part of several things which provide a framework for what you do but also provide a limit to what you can do. You are not alone.

The organizational context

Managers are part of an employing organization. There is a group of people, perhaps a very large group, who are linked together in a shared enterprise that has a name. The name is a part of the identity of all its members, as is their job title.

'This is Henry, he's a sound engineer with the BBC.' That brief introduction at a drinks party immediately begins a picture of Henry. He is a sound engineer, with all the attitudes to the engineering profession that other people carry in their heads. The BBC is a large organization with highly trained specialists. Henry's identity begins to take shape and within the BBC this is taken further by a linking together of jobs into particular sections and departments, with a further set of linkages between departments and an overarching hierarchy distributing authority and responsibility.

Some businesses use titles that rank people according to status. Universities have some people who are professors, some people who are senior lecturers and some lecturers who form a particular leading cadre of people in the business: academics. Strangely enough, academics tend to the opinion that they are also the most important. That form of categorization has a clear meaning for those who are in the university. Similar rankings are found in social work, in hospitals, schools and other bodies where there is a generally accepted purport of different titles used across a number of similar bodies, although outsiders may not understand them. How many people, for example, understand the distinction in journalism between a reporter and a correspondent? Some job titles can be puzzling. 'Unqualified Tutor' is a title for certain healthcare professionals to indicate that the person with the badge has not yet completed the programme of further specialist training to be fully qualified but they are still recognized as tutors. Some members of the public interpret the badge as meaning the holder is not qualified at all, or even disqualified.

In less status-ridden businesses there can be titles that make sense within the organization, but can puzzle outsiders. Rubber technician and plastic executive lead to all sorts of misunderstanding. A sales executive is usually someone who 10 years ago would have been a sales representative. This change is mainly to impress customers and to massage the ego of the representative/executive. An operative in an engineering factory is usually less skilled than a technician, who is less skilled than an engineer, but this distinction has more substance than the sales titles because it defines the limits of what the job holder is allowed to do. Another example is the distinction between a podiatrist and a podiatry assistant. The first has taken a higher qualification than the assistant. To Joe Public this means that a podiatry assistant can trim your toenails but cannot use a scalpel on your corns. Some job identities are enhanced by a uniform or badge. Someone wearing a high-visibility jacket with PARAMEDIC on the back will usually be given immediate access to the scene of a road accident, whereas someone in jeans and a hoodie is less readily welcome. Police officers not in uniform would normally announce their name and rank while producing a warrant card if calling at a private house.

KEY CONCEPT 8

Your job title tells people what you are; this is important. The title of the job you are doing gives you a recognized place and function in the various contexts and networks within which you work. This is a necessary prerequisite to effective working with clients and colleagues.

The economic context

The employing organization is part of an economy, local, regional, national and international. Butchers' shops are crucially dependent on the local economy as that is the situation from which most of their customers come. But they are also part of the economy of their region. Butchers in Cumbria, for instance, will probably welcome an advertisement encouraging Cumbria as a tourist destination, especially if an accompanying illustration includes a picture of the distinctive Cumbrian sausage. They are part of the national economy and its relative success or failure in contrast with the rest of the world.

The political context

Managers cannot escape the political context in which they work. Any business has to operate within its economic and political environment. This both constrains managerial freedom and assists managerial effectiveness. Managerial freedom is constrained by taxation, the current state of the economy, social planning and philosophy, and laws which prevent managers doing what they might wish. In managing with people, law will enshrine individual rights in employment to limit undue exploitation by managers and unreasonable behaviour by fellow employees. Managers can be aided in their effectiveness by employment services, conciliation services, training and grants. If your national economy is in difficulty but your particular business is flourishing, you cannot avoid the fact that your suppliers, customers and fellow citizens have difficulties that may make them envious or disapproving of your good fortune. This has been clearly demonstrated in the protests throughout the western world against what is seen as disproportionately high financial rewards for senior executives in businesses and especially in banks.

The social context

Chapter 4 deals with the formal structures in an organization while Chapter 5 deals with the less tangible but equally powerful social and cultural realities. The political context of a business can be likened to organizational structure in that it is deliberately formed and described by people. The social context is like the culture within a business. It is intangible but fundamental to the effective working of a society. It cannot be deliberately formed by people but its nature is the product of people's collective behaviour. Managers need to understand their social context as that will influence the attitudes and behaviour of employees who have to be selected, organized, motivated, led and rewarded. Employment legislation deals with rights and obligations universally. Within that framework managers know that some people in certain types of job will tend to be highly competitive and looking for individual incentives that would be counter-productive and unwelcome for other people attracted to other types of job.

Managers are empowered in some ways and constrained in others by laws and by economic realities, but they have to comply with social realities as well. They are expected to be good citizens, and these are the expectations of their colleagues at work, the friends and relatives of those colleagues and the expectations of the local community. An example is the treatment of those who are ill. The legal situation is clear: if a person is *not capable* of performing their duties, there are grounds for dismissal subject to reasonable safeguards according to local practice and natural justice. The social realities may be different. The 18-year-old male who rarely gets to work before 11.00 am for a 9.00 am start and then falls asleep by 2.00 pm having made a number of mistakes can be easily dismissed after due warnings. At the opposite extreme, managers will be most reluctant to dismiss someone with 20 years' experience who has long spells of absence with a serious illness.

Sir Fred Goodwin was a chartered accountant who was chief executive of the Royal Bank of Scotland Group (RBS) between 2001 and 2009. The early part of his time in that post was marked by rapid expansion until RBS was one of the largest companies in the world. With the onset of the credit crunch catastrophe in 2008, losses at RBS were a spectacular £24 billion, the largest ever in British history, and being 'too big to fail' RBS was effectively nationalized amid widespread criticism of the disastrous policies that had led to the failure.

In October 2008, Fred Goodwin announced his resignation as chief executive and early retirement to take effect in January 2009. In the following February it was revealed that his annual pension would be £700,000. Despite public outcry over a severance package that was regarded not only as gross by most standards but also a reward for total failure, Fred Goodwin resisted all suggestions that he should decline a substantial proportion, pointing out that it was not a negotiated or discretionary sum but one agreed some time before and set in a watertight, legally binding contract. His home was attacked and his family had to leave the country for a time, so eventually he did decline a token proportion. Later he became a pariah and had his knighthood removed.

The social context of the business always has a bearing on management by, and management of, the people within it.

The international context

Managing people usually has an international dimension, although the level varies.

A business that has interdependent manufacturing plants in different parts of the world engaged in different stages of producing the same product has a significant international dimension. We had a glimpse of this with Tina. Another example is Airbus, which has different parts of an aircraft made in different countries before final assembly in Toulouse, with all the potential problems of language barriers, national pride and different methods of working and programming. A hotel or a hospital is likely to have staff members of varying nationalities with different levels of facility in the language of the host nation and widely differing experience and training. These are the two types of business where the international dimension is most pronounced and potentially complex, but internationalism is steadily growing.

KEY CONCEPT 9

Managers are both enabled and restricted by their contexts: job title, economic, political, social, international.

Within these broader contexts the main arena in which the manager, whether with that title or not, operates is the employing organization. Aspects of managing to manage in this arena are explored in Chapters 3, 4 and 5, but here are two preliminary aspects to consider.

The bottom line

It's not within the scope of this book nor of my competence to pronounce on budgets, cash flow and other financial matters, but for managers there is always a bottom line. If you are a householder, a church or a charity, a public sector employee or part of a commercial business needing to make a profit, there is money for you to use but limits on what you can do with it and how much you can use.

All managers have responsibilities that incur costs. Some of those are lost in a general category of overheads, others are the responsibility of someone else in management, but most managers have some degree of personal responsibility for, and control of, specific aspects of expenditure. Exceeding the limit involves at least questions and possibly penalties, depending on the answers to the questions. *Force majeure* is a difficult answer to get away with, so if you argue that the customer is always right and therefore you had to authorize some compensation payments, you are likely to receive more questions, like where you are going to make economies elsewhere to meet some of the shortfall and what measures you have taken to ensure no repetition of the problem, which will inevitably be an issue in your upcoming annual appraisal. It is advisable to use your network before you incur an overrun. Your boss may find some way of mitigating the problem, not least by agreeing with what you propose to do. Other colleagues may accept that part of the difficulty is in their area.

Spending less than your budget allowance may bring a rare smile of approval from the commissar who would ask the sharp questions about overspend, but don't bank on it. You have the allowance for necessary expenditure, so make sure you have met all your targets and the expectations of others about your performance. You might not get one of those rare smiles if you have undershot your budget by economizing on essential sales training.

Entitlement

People at work are entitled to many things in connection with their work and many of them are obvious: reasonable safety and privacy, payment, holidays, fair dealing and so forth, but some of them are more difficult, like expenses and perquisites or 'perks'. If someone incurs necessary expenditure in fulfilling their obligations they would be entitled to reclaim their expenditure from their employer, but how much and for what? Staying overnight at a London hotel incurs expenditure. There is probably a company policy on the acceptable price range for bed and breakfast for which you can reasonably also claim for a wi-fi connection in your room, but what about the charge for watching a so-called adult film? You can claim the invoiced cost of an evening meal, but what about an accompanying bottle of wine?

All these questions are usually for the HR people to work out beforehand by setting policy guidelines for people to follow and some clear rules, like mileage allowance for using your own car. Over-dependence on inflexible rules leads to a bureaucratic nightmare with extensive books of guidance including an index. I have seen one such set of rules that was 84 pages long and the index did not work. There is no single best way, but the most effective general practice seems to be carefully drafted general guidelines on the most common matters that cannot be made absolute, like mileage allowance, and a limited list of people authorized to pass expense claims of others. The authorized claims then pass to a central person for approval and payment. The need for that final arbiter is to ensure reasonable consistency across the business.

Conditions of employment can cause interesting problems about who is entitled to what. A textiles company introduced a policy allowing employees up to three months' leave without pay in order to visit overseas family. This was in response to a request from employees with extended family in India, Pakistan or Bangladesh. Six weeks later they had an application from a long-serving English woman employee who had been recently widowed. She wished to travel to Australia to stay with her daughter, who was awaiting the delivery of her first child. At first the request was rejected as it was a policy intended only to apply to the three specific groups of employees. This was so patently discriminatory and unlawful that it was rapidly reversed.

Custom and practice in entitlement can be very difficult to alter. In an attempt to achieve a fair way of controlling uncertified sickness absence, some businesses have a policy that employees are entitled to *up to*, say, 10 days' such absence a year. In many cases the words 'up to' are ignored and departments are depopulated during the last few weeks before the end of the year. Another custom is to add a week of sick leave to a week of annual leave in order to take a fortnight's annual holiday.

In the days of the Central Electricity Generating Board, certain members of staff were entitled to no more than 10 days of uncertified sickness absence in each financial year, ending on 31 March. Passing through an engineering drawing office towards the end of March one year, you immediately saw that it was empty except for the chief draughtsman in his corner office. He explained that all the draughtsmen were 'getting in their sick leave'.

The manager is not alone

Managing is something everybody does all the time. Managing at work increases the amount of formality and the number of people with whom one has to interact. People with the word 'manager' in their job title usually have authority over some of the people they work with, as well as an area of responsibility. People without the word 'manager' in their title may still have that type of authority and responsibility. To understand where they are and what they can, and should, be doing they need to be aware of the ways in which the surroundings of their jobs both enable them to perform and limit their freedom.

Managing at work has various contexts. Most immediate is the employing organization which has formal arrangements and shared values within which individuals have to work. Beyond that is the political and economic context in which the employing organization sits and which produces other limitations and opportunities. There are legal requirements, issues of the marketplace, financial requirements and so forth. The social context is the product of the behaviour, values and attitudes of people in society at large. Much of this is within the organization itself, as its people bring in their values and behaviour from outside, but the broader aspects influence managerial action as well. The international dimension is a yet wider arena within which management takes place, but this varies considerably according to the nature of the business.

FURTHER READING

The broader context in which business operates is in Marr, A (2009) *A History of Modern Britain*, Macmillan, London. An older work is Sampson, A (1964) *The Anatomy of Britain*, Hodder & Stoughton, London, which is slightly stronger on the social dimension.

Chapter Three
How businesses work

Strategy, policy, procedures and targets

Any business works by using four broad types of mechanism to enable their people to work effectively together: strategy, policy, procedures and targets.

Strategy

This is the sexy beast because it is mainly the province of the people in the business who spend their time in creative or weighty discussion in comfortable surroundings thinking great thoughts and earning the most money. Other people envy them their perceived privileges while forgetting the risks involved in the responsibilities they discharge.

It is about knowing what you want to do and how you are going to get there. It seems blindingly obvious, but some businesses have a strategy that is unrealistic or has become unrealistic but they don't know how to change, or maybe they don't want to change.

Strategy has its origins in military activity and refers to a broad plan of action to achieve a particular objective, while tactics is about how you do it. In business strategy is similar, while tactics is seen as a mixture of policy and procedure. Targets can be deployed in both strategy and policy. Both are fundamental to the day-to-day workings of any business and its people, *who have to understand (not just know) what the strategy is.* If they are committed to that strategy, if they have played a part in it, that is even better, but not essential. Any strategy is likely to be unwelcome to some people for personal reasons and will rarely be good news for everyone; remember Key Concept 2.

Strategy has to be looking out to the market to be sure that what the business does is what some people need. One of the failures to do that was Sir Clive Sinclair, an inventor who produced the first mass-market pocket calculator and the first viable home computer. Both found a market and Clive Sinclair was a heroic innovator. His next venture was a small electric car. This was a great technical accomplishment but a commercial disaster: nobody wanted it and certainly nobody needed it. The key word is 'need' rather than 'want', as many successful innovators uncover a need that few people think they have. Lakeland Ltd is a medium-sized business marketing household items, including novel items. A common observation on the way to a Lakeland store is: 'I'm going for one or two things I want and will probably come away with something I don't yet know I need!'

From that starting point other strategic questions flow: Can we get the money? Have we got the resources? Have we got the expertise? How do we sell? How do we manufacture and supply? These all generate further issues that will shape the detail of strategic thinking.

KEY CONCEPT 10

Strategy describes the sense of purpose and overall direction of the business. It is developed with varying degrees of formality according to the size, complexity and ownership of the organization. It is forward-looking and must be realistic as well as motivating the necessary actions to realize the objectives.

Policy

Policy complements strategy by describing the way in which the objectives will be carried out. Reverting to the military model, 'Capture that hill' might be the strategy while a policy might be 'Take no prisoners'. Some of the main policies in a contemporary business relating to its people are about whether or not all vacancies will be advertised, the avoidance of unlawful discrimination, union recognition or not, health and safety, fairness in dismissal, methods of redundancy, and how people are paid. Other areas that impinge on members of the business and which are more recent are environment and ethics.

Developing policy is partly because of external influences, partly simple management instigation and partly a response to an employee request or complaint. The most obvious external influence is the law relating to employment. Dismissal is set about with a number of protections for the employee that are quite specific as well as some protection for the employer. The employee cannot, for instance, be dismissed without being given a reason and the opportunity to challenge the decision. Providing that due process is followed, an employer is able to dismiss someone for lack of capability to perform their duties, even if the incapability is due to severe illness. In practice most employers are very reluctant to dismiss someone who is seriously ill, first because the individual person taking the decision would not wish to and second because other people in the business would disapprove.

Ethical policies are easier if there is already an accepted code within a profession. If you employ a company medical officer, what you want that person to do will be dependent on the generally accepted code of ethics that doctors follow. They will not jeopardize their professional careers for managerial convenience. One feature of this code is that a practitioner should act in the best interest of the patient. If an employer wished to dismiss someone on the grounds of incapability due to illness, the medical officer might have difficulty in endorsing the decision unless convinced that it was in the best interest of the patient.

Throughout the 1990s a number of large companies produced written ethical policies covering employee affairs and relations with customers, ranging from the simple, 'Never knowingly undersold', to lengthy documents. These frequently included an environmental dimension following concerns about climate change and animal health.

In developing policy it is even more important than with strategy that those who have to implement the policy, or their representatives, are closely involved in its drafting. They will certainly find all manner of reasons why some aspects simply will not work, but they will also have excellent suggestions for improvement. Just make sure you get them hooked on the idea before you get on to the practice.

KEY CONCEPT 11

Policy complements strategy. Strategic thinking needs policies to make it happen and policies are also needed to ensure the business is conducted in a way that fits the organization within its evolving economic, political and social contexts.

Procedures

Strategy and policy are two sides of the same coin and it is sometimes difficult to know where one ends and the other begins. Procedures are different; they are the life blood of any organization, yet are scarcely ever discussed. Many books on general management extend over more than 500 pages but the term 'procedure' does not appear in the index. The reason they are ignored is that they are dull. The reason they are important is that things get done in any organization through the effective use of well-designed procedures. Exciting decisions may be taken, creative ideas may be developed, new products may be conceived, but all of them depend on organizational procedures to get things done.

In some businesses one major procedure is the key determinant of success or failure, like the procedure for booking seats in an airline company, or order processing and despatch in a mail order company, but in all organizations procedures are essential to success; they get things done.

Managers' lives are dominated by procedures and much of their creative energy is spent in trying to circumvent them or expedite processes through them. A popular managerial self-image is of the person who can 'beat the system' or 'get things done without waiting for procedures which always take such a hell of a long time'. The idea of procedures is such anathema to most managers that many readers will have passed over this section, but procedures efficiently expedite the great majority of action that takes place in the business. Lack of effective procedures produces uncertainty, reluctance to accept responsibility, inconsistent results and errors. Your pet project that you cannot wait to get going on might eventually be better if *all* the checks have been made and *all* the necessary expertise has been lined up.

There are obviously many occasions when procedure is not appropriate, like the apocryphal story of the man in the burning building who could not find the right requisition form for a fire extinguisher, but the impersonal, dead hand of administrative routine is the best way to put into practice the majority of the decisions taken within organizational structures. Managers need, therefore, to consider and design procedures with consummate care, so as to save money, so as to save time, and so as to run a successful operation. Writing 30 years ago, two Americans, in a book ignored in the UK these days, but still popular in Germany, summed it up neatly:

> Procedures... establish a customary method of handling future
> activities. They are truly guides to action, rather than to thinking,

and they detail the exact manner in which a certain activity must be accomplished. Their essence is chronological sequence of required actions. (Koontz, O'Donnell and Weihrich, 1980: 166)

Using procedures reduces the need for future decisions, like the cookery recipe, a routine that has worked before and will work again. The HR manager needing to fill a vacancy for a clerical assistant will similarly use a 'recipe' or standard operating procedure. It speeds up implementation because the decision making has been done before; it also provides the opportunities of efficiency through practice and a modest amount of de-skilling. The smooth procedure can be operated by those with less skill than the decision maker and procedure inventor, just as a million cooks can use a Jamie Oliver recipe.

From time to time there is an accident or some other scandal in a business that can perhaps be attributed to human error. After the shocked headlines in the press a spokesperson will produce a statement explaining that '… procedures have been reviewed to ensure this can never happen again'.

The relationship between procedure and policy is one needing careful understanding. A policy is a general statement of intention about how things will be done, for example:

1 We are going to switch our advertising from television to national dailies.

2 We are going to discontinue manufacture of …

3 We are an equal opportunity employer.

Each of those statements requires to be sold to members of the business before it can become effective, not only for them to be advised, but also for them to be convinced that the policy is appropriate, so that they will put it into practice with enthusiasm and thoroughness. The policy statements also, however, need procedures to make them work. Procedure is the link between policy and practice, and policies that fail may be poor decisions or good decisions that people elsewhere in the organization never understood, but most often they are good decisions that foundered because there was no procedural follow-through.

Procedures are consistent and most operations that are to be repeated benefit from being repeated in the same way, particularly when they involve other people who have to respond to the operation. Customers gradually become familiar with an organization's procedures and practices, so that they waste less of the organization's time if all staff treat them consistently. Staff become accustomed to a routine of departmental practice and are able to develop smooth interaction and swift handling if the method remains the same. Herein lies one of the great problems, as well as an advantage, of procedures: they are very difficult to alter and those who use them will abandon them only under duress. This is well illustrated in the field of industrial relations, where not adhering to procedure is the most heinous of crimes.

Procedures provide some autonomy for staff. Without procedure as a guideline, people have to await decisions from others. They have to be told how to do things as well as what to do, so that they remain dependent with little scope for individual action. Procedure authorizes and informs. Individuals know what to do and how to do it. In uncertainty they may ask a colleague, but they can also 'look it up'. Good procedure always provides scope for individual decision and action to interpret the rules in particular situations. The importance of close management attention to devising procedures is shown by the frequent problems that occur when they are poorly conceived or inappropriate. Poor procedures can be worse than no procedures at all as it is only the experts who can cope with them, usually through custom and practice, so that the relatively inexperienced are not authorized and informed, they are made dependent on the experts.

A final main advantage is that procedure is a means towards management control of operations. The delegation that was implicit in providing the autonomy mentioned above means that managers can turn their attention to other things, confident in the system that will keep things moving in the right general direction. There will be fewer requests for information and guidance, fewer complaints and errors, fewer worries about the minutiae of organizational life. At the same time as providing freedom from control for individual members of the organization, procedure provides effective control of operations to the management generally.

KEY CONCEPT 12

Procedures enable the right future to happen. They provide recipes for people to follow; they ensure consistency in the way things are done; they give autonomy to individuals; and they are a means of management control.

There are four common types of procedure: task performance, planning and expenditure authorization, information and coordination, and mutual control.

Task performance procedures

These are the most common. The ability of the skilled engineer to work to drawings is an ability to work to procedures. Other examples are the job description, which describes a job partly in order to explain to job holders what to do and how to do it; the training manual, which is used by the new recruit to acquire a knowledge of the routine which the job involves; the list of operations that are run through in closing down a plant; fire drill for evacuating the premises in cases of emergency.

Some task performance procedures are brought with them by trained, newly recruited personnel, as they are universal. The typist arrives knowing the procedures involved in producing a page of accurate typescript, the electrician arrives knowing how to wire a socket. Further task performance drills are specific to the organization in which they are carried out. The typist knows how to type, but does not know where to obtain supplies of paper and envelopes, where to put outgoing mail for despatch, nor a whole series of procedures relating to house style, number and destination of copies and so on. The accountant charged with pricing a product to ensure a proper return needs to know not only good practice in the accountancy profession and a technique for making the calculation, but also the organizational practice on credit in order to establish the appropriate criteria for the calculation.

An important subset of task performance drills are those concerned with changing the rules and coping with new situations. Legislation on electronic data protection was a simple idea that spawned innumerable one-day seminars, training packages and computer programs to explain it to managers. However, what was being explained was not the law, but devices for changing organizational procedures in task performance so that staff members did their routine operations in a different way. It was the daunting nature of that task that caused the managerial anxiety.

Planning and expenditure authorization procedures

These are mostly the responsibility of senior managers, but minor authorizations are replicated throughout the organization. Although long-range, corporate planning is not as comprehensive an activity as the writers of management books would have us believe; there is always some amount of planning which seeks to set goals and targets for achieving whatever the strategy is. The plan specifies not only the ultimate destination but also the intermediate steps to be reached on the way. A marketing plan would, for instance, specify not only a target market share of x by a stated date, but also steps of 25 per cent of x to be achieved by an earlier date, 50 per cent of x to be achieved six months later and 75 per cent to be reached six months after that. Such a plan is based on untested assumptions and is therefore theoretical, but provides a general operating framework that needs change and updating as circumstances evolve. The way in which the plan is given influence over the behaviour of organization members is by allocating resources and authorizing expenditure.

We are concerned here with the procedures of planning and expenditure authorization, rather than with planning methods, and the procedures of planning are unusual in the participative nature of their generation. Agreeing on the budget and setting operating plans are nearly always collaborative acts in which a range of interests are reconciled to obtain consensus support for the programme. Procedures for expenditure authorization are of two kinds. Setting the overall budgets is aligned with the planning agreements and probably follows the same procedures precisely, but authorizing items of expenditure against budget is an activity delegated to managers who have task performance rules for this procedure. Spending money is not just being allowed because your proposal has been accepted, but because you will be following the drills which check that the expenditure is in accordance with another set of rules on proper organizational behaviour.

Information and coordination procedures

These have a less precise objective in that a business can limp along without them, but performance is generally improved if people know what is going on and feel that they are kept in touch. Typically, information flows in from the outside of the business to the apex of the organization pyramid or to well-identified other places in the hierarchy. The method of passing information on to other members of the organization will lie in procedure, so that there is some semi-automatic means whereby dissemination takes place, rather than dependence on the individual recipient to take thought and decide on dissemination.

Among the procedures found for information and coordination are using minutes of meetings, which are often circulated to a wider group than just those who attended the meeting. If action is required by recipients there will be a note about who is expected to take action on the decisions made at the meeting.

Mutual control procedures

These enable the employer and the individual employee to exercise a degree of control over each other. Grievance and discipline procedures are the main examples, as the parties to the contract of employment have a series of procedural steps available to them so that they can limit, or alter, the actions of the other. More on this in Chapter 8.

Problems with procedures, and some solutions

Procedures present problems as well as opportunities, the most difficult of which is their dullness: 'Managers often fail to obtain the interest and support of top managers in the tedious and unromantic planning and control of procedures' (Koontz *et al*, 1980: 769).

That is difficult to resolve, but has to be recognized. Another problem is that they inhibit change. When they eventually become operational and everyone is used to them, they provide a comfortable, secure routine, an aspect of organizational maintenance where people can feel at home with the familiar. This is much like the way in which managers move from management to administrative activity when the management work gets too hectic, which we looked at earlier. There is always the risk that procedure becomes custom and practice and as immutable as the laws of the Medes and the Persians.

Overlapping and duplication cause problems when each section of the organization has its own procedures that do not quite coincide with those of other sections. Purchasing has procedures that are not quite the same as Accounts and both are quite different from those in Engineering. The varying emphasis is necessary, as accountants have different responsibilities from buyers. The problems come when the overlapping or duplication becomes too great.

A less obvious problem is when procedures are used to try to solve problems that require a policy solution. Procedures are needed to put policy into practice, but policies are needed for procedures to be effective. The HR manager in a small textile company was anxious to eradicate racial discrimination from personnel practice within the organization and made a number of procedural adjustments to this end. Standardized forms of words to be used in job advertisements were devised, instructions were given to telephonists about handling telephone enquiries, short-listing arrangements in the personnel office were altered and various other methods of preventing unfair discrimination were introduced. He failed, however, to explain these moves to anyone outside the department and was accused of high-handedness and deviousness by his colleagues. He also found that the procedural devices did not work: checks on advertisement wording were overlooked, departmental managers disagreed with short lists and there was a formal complaint to the Equality and Human Rights Commission. This was due to a lack of policy decision and commitment. The policy decision was made only in the HR manager's mind, being neither discussed with, nor communicated to, anyone else. The telephonists and personnel staff did not fully understand the reasons for the changes they had been asked to make and other managers did not understand what was being done. Once the policy was clear, sold and accepted, the procedure worked well. Procedure can only deal with organizational problems for which a procedural solution is appropriate.

Procedure is inherently rigid. A standard way of doing things risks being the only way of doing things. Grievance procedures nearly always specify that aggrieved employees should raise their dissatisfaction first with their immediate organizational superiors. This is for a number of very good reasons, such as to prevent the immediate superior being bypassed and to ensure that the matter will be resolved as quickly as possible and by the people most closely involved. Carried to an extreme, that could be interpreted as prohibiting an employee talking to a more senior manager about anything. When organizational change is needed, the rigidity of procedures can prove too much for the enthusiasm with which the change is sought.

A common problem is the complexity of procedures. This is where the procedural steps are intended to eliminate any discretion at all. Such procedures are difficult for people to remember and to understand, so that they may be used only by, literally, following the book. They also challenge the ingenuity of people who resist the lack of scope for personal judgement and interpretation. An example is in safe working procedures, which are regularly ignored by skilled and experienced operators who have sufficient skill and knowledge to do, safely, what would be highly dangerous for others.

KEY CONCEPT 13

Though essential, procedures can cause problems.

To overcome these difficulties, those designing procedures should always aim for simplicity, so that they can be readily understood by those who operate them and those who are affected by them, allowing scope for interpretation to suit particular circumstances. Procedures should always be as few as possible, so that there is less to remember and so that the degree of overlapping and duplication is limited. Also, a new procedure should not be introduced unless it is deemed really necessary. To be necessary, a series of future incidents has to be likely, so as to require some thought-out decisions in advance. Producing a procedure to deal with a situation that occurs seldom but with similar results is useful. Producing a procedure to deal with a situation which occurs seldom and with very varied results is pointless. Procedures should be tested to see if they meet their objectives. A hospital was receiving a number of complaints from patients' relatives, so a complaints procedure was set up. This had the unfortunate effect of lengthening the time taken to deal with complaints and increasing their number. We have to make sure not only that procedures have an internal logic, but also that they do what they are set up to do.

Procedures must have the before and after stages of policy and communication. There must be a policy for the procedure to implement, even if it is only the implicit policy of established practice, and all affected must know what the procedure is. 'Knowing' is not the same as 'being told about'.

Monitoring can prevent procedures becoming obsolete and inefficient. Not only must they be communicated, they must also be monitored in operation to make sure that they are being worked properly and that there are no unintended effects that should be smoothed out before too much damage is done.

Targets

The twenty-first century has seen an explosion in the use of targets in businesses and organizations of all sorts. The past 20 years have seen an almost exponential rise in the bonuses received by senior bankers during a time of economic austerity. Almost everyone, except senior bankers, believes that the level of the bonuses is too high. The second illustration demonstrates the problem of a target being linked to payment. It has to be achievable, specific and not dependent on someone's judgement. If it is not achievable and specific, the person hoping for the money will not make the requisite effort. If it depends on the judgement of someone else and the hoped-for payment is not made, it is deemed not fair, and might even lead to a claim for constructive dismissal. The more specific the target, the greater the risk of all effort being expended on reaching it and possibly neglecting other aspects of the role. In certain cases it is not sufficient to have a target that is specific and measurable; change in circumstances may make it unacceptable, as with some directors' bonuses that shareholders have rejected.

Target setting in any but the smallest business is difficult, very difficult if you attach money. The simplest situation is the one person writing a book or a song. The author contracts with a publisher to produce the work in exchange for a royalty agreement of x per cent of the publisher's income from selling the work. If the published work is a runaway success the author will probably be satisfied; if it fails the author will be distraught and will grumble bitterly to family and friends about the incompetence and indolence of the publisher, but to no avail. It was an accepted risk for both parties and both must live with the disappointment. In a business, success is produced by cooperative effort. How do you reward individuals fairly and effectively to engineer the appropriate result? If the issue is not success but failure, the problem is greater.

KEY CONCEPT 14

Too often targets generate the wrong behaviour. Either the targets become misaligned with the behaviour needed in a changing situation, or the behaviour is too narrowly focused on the target at the expense of the wholeness of the job to be done.

Reference

Koontz, H, O'Donnell, C and Weihrich, H (1980) *Management*, 7th edn, McGraw-Hill, New York.

FURTHER READING

There are two significant authorities on strategy: Michael Porter and Henry Mintzberg, who have slightly different views. Try Porter, ME (2004) *Competitive Strategy: Techniques for analysing industries and competitors*, Free Press, New York, and Mintzberg, H (1994) *The Rise and Fall of Strategic Planning*, Free Press, New York, or Moore, K (2011) Porter or Mintzberg: whose view of strategy is the most relevant today?, *Forbes Magazine*, March.

I have not been able to find a source for further reading on procedures in general, because they are mainly a matter of carefully applied common sense. Two specific methods that can be used to achieve the best sequence in complex procedures are critical path analysis and linear programming. A recent text is Wisniewski, M and Klein, J (2001) *Critical Path Analysis and Linear Programming*, Palgrave Macmillan, London.

A source for employment procedures is Cushway, B (2012) *The Employer's Handbook 2012–13: An essential guide to employment law, personnel policies and procedures*, Institute of Directors, London.

Chapter Four
Organization structure

The whole thing, your bit of it and you

Hierarchy is much misunderstood, and is frequently used to refer vaguely to those terrible people in charge who are always making a mess of things. But hierarchy is necessary in any but the smallest businesses. It was essential to building the Egyptian pyramids, to maintaining army discipline, to avoiding corruption in civil administration, and to running any medium to large business.

In science a hierarchy is a classification of ordered groupings, such as the arrangement of plants and animals into classes, orders, families and so forth. In management, hierarchy is very similar. The American writer Harold Leavitt got it dead right 40 years ago:

> The hierarchy is the chain of command, the pyramid of authority that narrows at the top ... if we eliminate all the paraphernalia of rank and authority in large organizations, we don't really know what we would end up with. There are no clear examples of large human organizations that operate without a formal hierarchy ... some form of hierarchy is *necessary* for organizing a complex set of people and resources. (Leavitt *et al*, 1973: 31–32)

He was describing the world of corporate business, mainly companies employing a lot of people. Although some form of hierarchy remains the norm, there are notable exceptions. Apple is one of the largest and most successful companies, yet it decries formal hierarchy and operates with small groups of engineers engaged in creative thinking and technological innovation. Managers who are not engineers are very rare, they will certainly not manage engineers and the possession of an MBA is almost a disqualification for working there. Companies in the creative industries generally dislike hierarchy, but few avoid it completely.

Rigid hierarchy can frustrate initiative and inhibit change so we now see less emphasis on formal hierarchy in business, with ideas like de-layering, loose structures, informality, breaking down barriers, open plan offices, self-managing groups and much more emphasis on the importance of organization culture: the soft and intangible as well as the hard and specific. We look at culture shortly, but hierarchy is still with us and the semi-formal structure of working relationships is still an intrinsic feature of all but the most esoteric and exciting types of business. Why should this be?

A *system* of roles and jobs is much more predictable than a simple gathering of people. It helps us understand how to get things done and how matters will be handled. To claim your expenses you want to know which job holder (not which person) pays out the money and which job holder authorizes the payment, as the organizational structure or system governs the behaviour of those job holders. Expenses are authorized within guidelines that people authorizing the payments can interpret but not ignore. The person paying out the money may dislike you, but is obliged by the system to pay you the money.

Hierarchy also distributes *power*, rations power and ensures that people accept the power of others in the system. Power is a word that has difficult overtones, as we tend to associate it with coercion and oppression. Lord Acton was a distinguished historian and moralist of the nineteenth century who is almost forgotten except for a single epigram which remains chillingly apt: 'Power tends to corrupt, and absolute power corrupts absolutely. Great men are almost always bad men.'

Hierarchy limits the tendency to corrupt at the same time as giving people the necessary authority to get things done, like settling your expenses. Holders of specified roles or jobs are empowered to make certain decisions and to control the behaviour of other people; power is distributed and rationed. Job holders can only exercise their ration of power as long as they accept the power invested in others; they must obey as well as direct. The clearest example of this is in the military, where the non-commissioned officer can direct soldiers to do certain things, and the soldiers risk severe punishment if they disobey. In turn, the non-commissioned officers enjoy that degree of authority only as long as they accept and obey the authority of other officers who outrank them. The reasons for have been summed up, again by Harold Leavitt:

> The formal hierarchy of authority serves several useful purposes, however imperfectly: (1) It supplements the informal power of individuals, helping even little men perform big jobs. (2) It provides control, order and predictability. (3) It helps to institutionalize the organization. (4) It helps to control and limit conflict. (Leavitt *et al*, 1973: 35)

Organizational fundamentals

Organizational structure deploys both *differentiation* and *integration*. Differentiation ensures that an individual job or task is undertaken effectively, while integration coordinates the output of the individual people so that the whole task is completed satisfactorily. Organizing individual jobs varies according to the degree of predictability in what has to be done, so that organizing of manufacturing jobs or a call centre tends to emphasize strict compliance with the rules, clearly defined tasks and much specialization. In a television programme about factory life, one man said this:

> I want the supervisor to tell me exactly what he wants me to do, no ifs or buts or well, what do you think? I want him to tell me straight and clear, and I will carry that out to the letter. Then I'm in the clear. If it's not right, and it hardly ever is, then it's his arse getting kicked, not mine.

That may sound very depressing and unliberated, but the nature of many manufacturing jobs leads in that direction.

Jobs which constantly present fresh problems and unpredictable requirements, like marketing and social work, produce frequent redefinition of job boundaries, a tendency to flexible networks of working relationships rather than a clear hierarchy and a greater degree of individual autonomy, but individual responsibility and accountability have to be clear. Unfortunately, this inevitably leads to writing down what was done, or what one intends to do, which is so often time-consuming and frustrating for those who are keen to get on with what they see as their real job.

The integrating process is influenced by the amount of differentiation. The greater the differentiation, the harder the task of coordination. Differentiation and integration produce a working organization by two complementary processes: *job definition* and *structure*.

We have already seen the importance of a job holder's title. More explanatory detail is set out in a job description or role definition. It is a valuable device for allocating people to jobs and tasks to people in a way that can be understood and for avoiding gaps and duplication, but you always need to think it through so that you describe a real job with a clear and sensible purpose. Occasionally a job is created in a hurry in order to shuffle off onto someone else a responsibility that is not well understood and probably unwelcome. Two recent classics have been the equality person and the health and safety person.

These can easily create a role without any power, understanding or influence and which is therefore ineffective apart from by force of personality.

KEY CONCEPT 15

Hierarchy works because: (a) a system of roles and jobs is more predictable that a gathering of people; (b) it distributes and rations necessary power; (c) it controls and limits conflict; (d) it works through differentiation and integration.

There is no ideal organizational structure. What works in one situation will be useless in another, but three broad types are common.

Entrepreneurial form relies on central power, like the spider's web, with one person or group so dominant that all power stems from the centre, all decisions are made at the centre and all behaviour reflects expectations of the centre. There are few collective decisions and much reliance on individuals, with actions stemming from obtaining the approval of key figures. It is frequently found in businesses where decisions must be made quickly and with flair and judgement rather than careful deliberation. Newspaper editing has an entrepreneurial form of organization and most of the performing arts have strong centralized direction. This seems to be the Apple model, although the company remains very secretive about this.

This is the form of most small and growing businesses as they owe their existence to the expertise or initiative of one or two people, and it is only by reflecting accurately that originality that the business can thrive. As the business expands, this type of structure can become unwieldy because too many peripheral decisions cannot be made without approval from the centre, which then becomes overloaded. It is also difficult to maintain if the spider leaves the centre of the web, as a successor may not have the same degree of dominance. In some instances the problem of increasing size has been dealt with by maintaining entrepreneurial structure at the core of the enterprise and giving considerable independence to satellite organizations, providing that overall performance targets are met.

An extreme example is the entourage surrounding a celebrity. An entertainer of international reputation may employ dozens of people, but the sole purpose of their employment is to sustain and extend the reputation of the spider at the centre of their web. If that person dies, the whole surrounding organization rapidly unravels, having lost its reason for existence. Less unusual examples are in financial services, where a fund manager's team may collapse if that person leaves, or in a school, where the tone of all that is done is largely determined by the head teacher.

Bureaucratic form emphasizes the distribution rather than centralization of power and responsibility: a more extended and complex hierarchy. It has been the conventional means of enabling an organization to grow beyond the entrepreneurial form to establish an existence that is not dependent on a single person or group of founders. Disney is a classic example of how a business, originally totally dependent on the flair of its founder, developed, expanded and diversified despite the demise of Walt Disney. Through emphasizing role rather than flair, operational processes become more predictable and consistent, with procedure and committee replacing individual judgement. Responsibility is devolved through the structure and it is a method of organization well suited to stable situations, making possible economies of scale and the benefits of specialization. There is seldom the flexibility to deal with a volatile environment and a tendency to be self-sufficient. 'Bureaucracy' is definitely a dirty word, so companies work hard at overcoming its drawbacks.

Matrix emphasizes the coordination of expertise into project-oriented groups of people with individual responsibility. It has been developed to counter some of the difficulties of the entrepreneurial and bureaucratic forms, first in the United States during the 1960s as a means of satisfying the government on the progress of orders placed with contractors for the supply of defence material. Checking on progress proved very difficult with a bureaucracy, so it was made a condition of contracts that the contractor should appoint a project manager with responsibility for meeting the delivery commitments and keeping the project within budget. In this way the government was able to deal with a single representative rather than with a number of people with only partial responsibility. The contractors then had to realign their organization so that the project manager could actually exercise the degree of control necessary to make the responsibility effective. This is done either by appointing a product manager with considerable status and power, or by creating product teams with specialists seconded from each functional area. The first method leaves the weight of authority with the functional hierarchy, while the product managers have a mainly coordinating, progress-chasing role as lone specialists. The second method shifts power towards the product managers, who then have their own teams of experts, with the functional areas being seen as a resource rather than the centre of action and decision.

Matrix is the form that appeals to many managers because it is theoretically based on expertise and provides scope for people at relatively humble levels of the business to deploy their skills and carry responsibility. It has, however, recently lost favour because it can generate expensive support systems for product managers needing additional secretaries, assistants and all the panoply of office, as well as the unwieldy administration referred to above.

This threefold classification is a means of analysis rather than a description of three distinct types of organization, with any undertaking being clearly one of the three. Bureaucracies will typically have matrix features at some points and few entrepreneurial structures are quite as 'pure' as implied here. Most large organizations could have one form dominant in one section of the business and another form dominant elsewhere.

Large banks, for example, are bureaucratic in their retailing operations as consistency is of paramount importance and any changes need to be put into operation simultaneously by a large number of people while being comprehensible to a large number of customers. The same banks will, however, tend to an entrepreneurial emphasis in their merchant banking activities and in currency dealings. The financial woes of 2008 and beyond could be largely attributed to an imbalance between the independence of the front-line risk takers and the authority of the back office bureaucrats.

KEY CONCEPT 16

Three broad forms of structure are: (a) entrepreneurial to emphasize central power; (b) bureaucratic to distribute power in a complex business; (c) matrix to coordinate diverse expertise.

Although variations of these types of organization are currently the most common, there are circumstances where there is a need for greater flexibility owing to the accelerating speed of change.

Big is no longer always beautiful. Most organizational structures evolved on an implicit assumption that the business would expand, but this is no longer seen as the sole form of growth: diversification and change are equally interesting, and sometimes wiser, alternatives.

The proliferation of expertise. Running a business requires an increasing variety of skills and diverse expertise, so that management relies on people knowing what to do and being required to get on with it. Seldom is a single business big enough to employ all the experts it requires, so many skills have to be bought in on a temporary basis from consultants or contractors.

Information technology. Increasingly computerized management information systems are able to produce the quality of control data that can de-personalize the management process to a great extent. Objectives for individuals and sections have a greater degree of quantification and performance is measurable. This does not always mean that the objectives are appropriate, nor that the measurement is correct!

Running alongside this is the practice of teleworking, whereby some of the people in the business work either from or at home, maintaining contact with the centre and with other colleagues by mobile phone, e-mail, fax, computer networking and computer conferencing. Working completely *at* home is not widely popular as most people feel a need for the direct contact, socialization, understanding and stimulus which can only come from meeting people face to face and participating in the multitude of interpersonal interactions that a business needs to drive itself forwards. Working *from* home is more attractive to many, and an interim position is what is sometimes called tele-cottaging, where you spend part of your time in the office at 'work' and part of your time in your 'office' at home. At the moment a slightly different change is the smartphone, which combines all the advantages of the old hand-held personal organizer with access to the internet. Theoretically this enhances the capacity of people to operate effectively while being physically remote from colleagues and workplace.

Centralization and decentralization

A popular idea of the 1980s was the strategic business unit. The management of a particular unit was given an agreed budget and an agreed set of targets for the forthcoming period. Thereafter they had freedom to manage themselves in whatever way they thought fit, providing that they first of all submitted regular reports and second that they met the targets and complied with the budget expectations. This is a form of decentralization, and many managers in strategic business units make the wry comment that the one thing that is not decentralized is the strategy!

What is to be decentralized and what is to remain central or drawn into the centre? In the process of a business decentralizing its operations, personnel or HR often remains one of the last centralizing forces because of central concerns about issues such as equity, order, consistency and control. The HR function will relinquish these reluctantly as they see great risks in, for instance, methods of payment being set up on different principles in separate parts of the business. They fear not only coercive comparisons between different groups of employees, but also problems such as falling foul of the law on such matters as avoiding discrimination.

In international companies managers have to centralize and decentralize at the same time, but it does not need the international dimension to make this comment valid. Each component part of the business has to have its strengths and knowledge developed and exploited to the full if it is to be effective, and this requires a greater degree of empowerment than most advocates of budget-driven strategic business units acknowledge. At the same time the individual operating unit has to maximize its contribution to group objectives, and that will inevitably lead to occasional profound conflict between unit and group objectives. The challenge in that is somehow to develop a culture that succeeds in delivering the apparently irreconcilable requirements: enough autonomy for people to deploy their skills, enthusiasm and commitment, but enough control for group-wide considerations ultimately to prevail. The organization must operate holistically. It is not the sum of its parts: the whole exists in every part, like the human body. If you are ill, a sample of your blood or the taking of your temperature is just as good an indicator to a doctor wherever it comes from. Customers have a holistic view of the organization because they are interested in what it delivers as a product or service, not in whether the design section is more efficient than the warehouse. Managers cannot work effectively in their part of the business without understanding its simultaneous relationship to the whole. Businesses function holistically and holism is a function of efficient communication (like the bloodstream) and control (like the central nervous system).

The organization of individual departments

Everyone remembers the disasters in Japan in 2011 and at Chernobyl in 1986. In 1979 there was nearly a disaster of similar catastrophic proportions in the nuclear reactor at Three Mile Island, near Harrisburg, the capital of Pennsylvania, when the reactor came very close to meltdown. Charles Perrow investigated this accident and concluded that it had nothing to do with the design of the reactor itself, but was due to the unsatisfactory features of the way individual jobs of the operators were organized (Perrow, 1985). The overall structure of the organization is important, but the organization of individual jobs and their interconnection within individual departments is equally important.

'Department' designates a distinct area, division, or branch of an enterprise over which a manager has authority for the performance of specified activities. Most departmental organization is intuitive rather than analytical, but there is a logical sequence that can be followed, as described below.

The *purpose* of creating a department may be a basic organizational objective, such as manufacture, or customer care, or maintenance, or it may be to make things run more smoothly. A common example is a systems department to interface between the people in the business and the information technology that processes data. Those who understand the electronic gadgetry are grouped together because of a skill they have in common. A countervailing argument is that it is better for skills to be dispersed. Matrix patterns of organization go part of the way towards this. Once a skills-based department is established, there are the risks of it being separated from the mainstream, aloof and having problems of communication. An alternative to organization on the basis of skills in common is to group people in departments on the basis of frequent contact. The obvious example is the grouping of secretaries, PAs and data input personnel. If they are all together in a secretarial services department there are the benefits of flexibility, shared facilities, specialized supervision and general economies of scale. On the other hand, if they are located individually with the people with whom they work, there are the advantages of easy access for receiving instructions, providing information, and a wider range of duties.

Once the purpose of the department has been decided, the next step is to decide on the *activities* it is to undertake, and here we have another boundary issue. How far is a new systems department to go in assuming the responsibilities that were previously distributed to others? What will the department do, and what will it not do? Then there are the questions about what types of people are needed with what types of expertise.

Jobs do not just happen; they are designed, even though the design process may be rather casual. Job design is putting together a range of tasks, duties and responsibilities to create a composite for individuals to undertake in their work and to regard as their own. Not only is that the basis of individual satisfaction and achievement at work, it is necessary to get the job done efficiently, economically, reliably and safely. Some of the job dimensions begin with the reasons for people to be employed in a particular organization. Consider, for example, employees in a large store.

Shop assistants are employed for product market reasons. The customer expects some type of sales service, ranging from detailed advice and technical explanation to simple cash-and-wrap operations. This is why shop assistants have to be on view, standing, identifiable and willing to interact constructively with even the most irritating of customers. The technology of the product produces further aspects of how the job is designed. Cosmetic saleswomen always wear what they sell; carpet salespeople spend much of their time lugging their products around, so dress accordingly. Others are employed for administrative reasons and the administrative structure will be the main influence on their jobs, so that payroll administrators spend most of their time sitting and doing solo manipulations with figures while buyers spend most of their time not buying at all but filling in forms to get the right balance between materials bought and materials sold.

Others are employed for social system reasons and a particular aspect of the social system determines the main dimensions of their jobs. The fire officer wears a special uniform so that people will respond in times of emergency. Catering staff have to fit in with the grossly inefficient timescale of their operations: intense activity around tea breaks and lunchtime.

Part of the management process is to mediate operational constraints and requirements like these in dividing work up between members of the organization, so that there are a number of composites, or jobs, that employees will be motivated to undertake and that are combined in such a way as to produce satisfactory working performance in the coordinated effort of the department and the organization.

Much of the interest in job design has centred round attempts to improve employee satisfaction with the working situation. It is inappropriate, however, to regard this type of initiative as only suitable for mass-production jobs. Administrative and managerial jobs, especially in large businesses, can be crying out for job design initiatives. Creating opportunities for senior managers can all too often involve limiting the scope of middle and junior managers to such an extent that the initiatives of their seniors are jeopardized.

Allocating *authority* in departmental organization enables staff to trigger other processes in the business by delegating authority to them, so that they are recognized as being authorized to act. One familiar method is the job description and its definition of boundaries, but other methods can be simpler and more effective in some circumstances. Being authorized to sign documents is one way of giving power to subordinates. If material cannot be issued from stores until Mr Jones has initialled the docket, then Mr Jones is clearly and effectively given that authority. Knowledge of passwords, computer codes, and possession of keys to the safe are similar allocations of authority. These specific and useful arrangements are not to be confused with status symbols, like whether or not you have a company car.

The department organization is finally made to work by the *connections* or means of communication between the members. Standard methods are e-mail, multiple copies of memoranda, meetings and departmental drills specifying the routing of paperwork or other material undergoing transformation. Less obvious is office landscaping, considering how closely people should work together and who should be next to whom.

Those who are constantly swapping items between them, who share a skill and need regular interaction, should probably sit together. A set of records to which four different people regularly refer should logically be equally accessible to each of them. There are many ways in which the layout of the working positions of people can aid the communication between them, but this is always limited by the social needs and expectations of employees. Very few people indeed really need an office to themselves and the private office is an impediment to communication, yet the interest in privacy and status is such that many people regard it as a basic requirement.

KEY CONCEPT 17

The organization of departments has two elements: (a) grouping people mainly according to complementary skills or organizational efficiency; (b) organizing people according to their activities, their jobs, the authority they need and the connections between them.

You may regard all this as hopelessly idealistic as most departments are just the way they are. People know what they are doing; they deliver the goods and for goodness sake don't shake it all up. Alternatively you may feel it is hopelessly mechanistic and rigid. However, some departments or units have to be set up from scratch, and some are so inefficient that life for the people doing the work is frustrating and they yearn for some improvement.

References

Leavitt, HJ, Dill, WR and Eyrig, HB (1973) *The Organizational World*, Harcourt Brace Jovanovich, New York.

Perrow, C (1985) *Normal Accidents*, The Free Press, New York.

FURTHER READING

Drucker, PF (1988) The coming of the new organization, *Harvard Business Review*, **66** (1), January–February. Drucker is always a good read. This article sets out his idea of the manager as the conductor of an orchestra. It is in stark contrast to the Apple approach.

Handy, CB (1993) *Understanding Organizations*, 4th edn, Penguin, Harmondsworth. Charles Handy is the British Drucker and shares with him the distinction of being rated as one of the 50 leading thinkers on management in the world. Here he discusses the different forms of organization, using language different from mine.

Chapter Five
Organization

The culture you work in

In the last chapter I referred to the shortcomings of hierarchy and formal organization structure. It seems to be necessary, but is not sufficient, for an organization to be able to succeed. Something else, intangible and difficult to define, makes all the difference. In the Second World War, RAF squadrons of fighter aircraft and their personnel were relatively informal in the way they behaved, with a creative approach to such things as uniform. In contrast, the Coldstream Guards regarded tight, formal discipline and strict adherence to the minute, detailed requirements of uniform as essential. Both groups were among the most effective military units in the world. They were both bound by the same King's Regulations and both on the same side in the same war. Both had very high morale and a high rate of applications to join, yet the way in which they behaved and worked was very different.

These differences were rooted in the nature of their work. Fighter pilots killed their opponents alone and relied on individual flair and courage. The Guards operated as integrated units, where the requirement to win the battle and to stay alive came from an acceptance of the fact that you instantly obeyed orders without question. Contemporary organizations are similar in having varying norms of behaviour. Accountancy companies are typically staffed by formally dressed people, who quietly get on with their jobs. Advertising agencies employ people tending to greater variety of dress and spend a great deal of time in creative tension, including turbulent working relationships. In a university a group of physicists will generally behave in a completely different way from a group of social scientists.

This type of variation is what management scholars have tried to capture by developing the concept of culture, the 'soft', energizing and intangible aspect of organizations that makes them function in such a variety of ways. Organizational culture is the characteristic spirit and belief in an organization, demonstrated, for example, in the norms and values that are generally held about how people should behave and treat each other, the nature of working relationships that should be developed and attitudes to change. These norms are deep, taken-for-granted, assumptions that are not always expressed, and are often known without being understood.

For a time, there was great interest in organizational culture as the key to improved organizational effectiveness; the counterbalance to the earlier preoccupation with structure. Organization charts may be useful in clarifying reporting relations and subtleties of seniority, but the culture or ethos of the business is an equally important determinant of effectiveness. Just as the development of matrix organizations was an attempt to reduce the rigidity of structure, so the interest in culture was an attempt to achieve the same objective, but by redefining the problem.

The history and traditions of a business reveal something of its culture because cultural norms develop over a relatively long period, with layers of practice both modifying and consolidating the norms and providing the framework of ritual and convention in which people feel secure, once they have internalized its elements.

Even when there are no obvious differences in the nature of the business and activities of two similar businesses, there can still be marked differences in culture.

KEY CONCEPT 18

The culture of a business is shared values and behaviour. Employees need to understand the culture so that they can adapt to it. Managers need to work within the culture in order to produce effective working.

Corporate culture

Organizational culture is the result of how an organization has developed; corporate culture is a more self-conscious expression of specific types of objective in relation to behaviour and values. This entices customers to buy, it entices prospective employees to seek jobs and causes them to feel commitment to the organization. This identity can be expressed and reinforced in various ways, such as a formal mission statement that is framed and hung in the entrance, or in such comments as 'we don't do things that way here'. There is the logo, the stationery, the uniform. In one way or another it is an attempt to ensure commitment. In all employing organizations there is less than total cooperation by members of staff, even where they accept the authority of managers and their right to manage. This is partly because managers have an unrealistic expectation about cooperation and partly because of the limited extent to which the authority of their position can be exercised. Even in the Coldstream Guards there has to be much more than simple instructions to obey if those in charge are to win the whole-hearted cooperation of their subordinates. Corporate culture can get round this problem by generating an atmosphere in which enthusiastic commitment is a shared norm.

Understanding organizational culture

Making sense of organizational culture depends as heavily on language as does wine connoisseurship, because it is always an attempt to grasp at something intangible. In describing structures you can draw the set of hierarchical relationships and produce an organization chart. In describing cultures you are left with metaphors:

1 Organizations are no longer described by what they produce or do; they have mission statements instead.

2 Mission statements are meant to 'cascade down' the organization and are the means of individual empowerment.

3 This empowerment in turn leads to great teams who run hot, who play passionately (even chaotically), towards the corporate mission, united in their common vision.

4 Managers are now re-conceived as 'heroes', 'great' and seeing every problem as an opportunity.

All of this is very good fun and it enables managers to escape from the tedious routine of 'getting things out by Friday' into a nice, fluffy world of academic discussion and redefinition of terms. This is not to disparage interest in culture, as it is real and powerful, however intangible. Those employed in an organization should try to understand the culture they share. They have to understand the extent to which culture can be changed and how the changes can be made, even if the changes may be much harder and slower to make than most managers believe and most circumstances allow. People who unwittingly work counter-culturally will find that they are impeded in trying to get things done. If they take the time to work out the nature of the culture in which they are operating, they can at least begin the process of change and influence the direction of the cultural evolution.

No organization is an island, so attempts to foster or alter corporate culture must take account not only of the intentions of those in charge and the expectations of those employed, but also of developments in the surrounding society, both nationally and internationally.

In Britain the idea of an enterprise culture in the 1980s was more than the platform of a political party, it was the expression of an idea whose time had come. There was a sudden upsurge of new businesses, mostly small and specialized, but there was also an associated change in values and expectations among many working people, especially the young, which was to increase interest in careers, mentoring, customized pay arrangements, networking and others. Whatever business you were in, you had to take on board this change of cultural emphasis. By the early 1990s, the enterprise emphasis had lost some of its momentum, although people remained more willing to take risks in order to get what they wanted out of life. By 2011–12 a greatly changed economic environment, as well as a change of government, had brought another boost to enterprise and a search for entrepreneurs.

Concern for the environment has developed steadily, so that the expression of environmental responsibility by a company is becoming necessary in the product market, but it is also necessary as a feature of the corporate culture to which employees will respond. It is becoming more difficult to get people to commit themselves to projects that they regard as environmentally unworthy. They may do it for the money, but will not offer commitment. Increasingly, people look to their workplace for their personal opportunities to do what is worthwhile. The extraordinary success of such television spectaculars as *Comic Relief* and *Children in Need* has been largely built on money raised by groups of people operating in, or from, their place of work.

Concern for the environment is growing at the national political level. At the local level there is not only concern about the ozone layer and climate change, but noise, dirt, smells and inconvenience to fellow citizens. Building developments, like new motorways, are vigorously resisted where there is to be a significant loss of green land. Corporate culture has to be attuned to these concerns.

Body Shop International is a business that has a most distinctive organizational culture that set it apart from most of its competitors when it started out in 1976. Superficially it seems like a boutique cosmetics company, yet its emphasis is on health and social responsibility rather than glamour and artificiality. Its products are 'to cleanse and polish the skin' rather than cover its blemishes. There was no consumer advertising, but financial commitment to social activism which, in turn, produced considerable media coverage and consequent sales. Much of this was centred on the founder and managing director, Dame Anita Roddick, who opened her first shop in 1976 so that she would be able to support herself and her children while her husband fulfilled a long-term ambition to ride from Buenos Aires to New York on horseback. Although Anita Roddick died in 2007, Body Shop continues with its original emphasis.

The marketing of the company is directed predominantly at women and generates enthusiastic commitment from most of its staff.

Developing organizational culture

As well as understanding the culture of which we are a part, we also need to understand how it can be developed or changed. In some ways Anita Roddick's job was easy. Having decided on a way of operating that was distinctive, she simply unleashed the power of her formidable personality and won a huge response in a situation where there was no tradition, no history. The culture had to be created, not altered. Most people are employed in undertakings with set norms and values, well-established ways of doing things. Not only do members of the organization find comfort in that familiarity, they also feel that something which 'has stood the test of time' must be the right way to do things. Tradition is 'hallowed' and not to be interfered with.

One of the most familiar cultural developments that many businesses have faced since the 1980s has been to increase customer orientation. Until then, it was a widespread notion that managers ran the business and sales representatives sold the product to customers. Management was concerned principally with the internal dynamics of the organization and technological innovation was either to make production more efficient or because it was interesting; the customer was somewhere else, and the marketing people were a different breed, wearing sharp suits and driving company cars that they did not deserve.

Many years ago I worked in a manufacturing company, where each of the supervisors worked hard to accumulate a 'backlog'. When there was a large number of unfilled orders, they felt that they had controlled the uncertainty of input sufficiently to 'set out their stalls' to keep production running smoothly, calling forward orders for completion that fitted in with their need for a steady flow rather than the date of the order or the urgency of the customer's requirements.

It has long been recognized that attitudes are harder to change than behaviour: actually trying a free sample of a new detergent is much more likely to make you believe it is better than lengthy explanation of its virtues. In developing corporate culture we have to start with trying to change norms of behaviour; over time those changed behaviours may lead to a change in the more deeply held beliefs of shared norms. Customer care is a good example. Company trainers may go to great lengths to explain the value of customers and their allegiance, but it is often quicker simply to tell staff what to say and how to handle queries or complaints. That can produce the cringe-making robotic behaviour of some telephone sales people ('Hello, is that Mr Smith? This is XYZ Ltd, Mandy speaking. Just a courtesy call. We make widgets and I would like to take just a few minutes of your time to tell you something about our latest line…'), but in face-to-face situations it can produce a friendly reaction from the customer. When the behaviour pays off, the attitudes and beliefs gradually shift.

An early analysis of organizational culture was by Schein (1985), who distinguished between the ways in which an organization needs to develop a culture which enables it to adapt to its changing environment and, at the same time, build and maintain itself through processes of internal integration. He suggests that cultures change and become consolidated by both primary and secondary mechanisms. The primary mechanisms are:

a what leaders pay most attention to;

b how leaders react to crises and critical incidents;

c role modelling, teaching and coaching by leaders;

d criteria for allocating rewards and determining status; and

e criteria for selection, promotion and termination.

This places great emphasis on example setting by those in leadership roles. If the manager walks round a construction site without a hard hat, it is unlikely that other people will regard such headgear as important. The comment about how leaders react to crises and critical incidents is interesting. At one level this is to do with reactions like calmness or urgency, but it is also a question of what is identified by leaders as crises and critical incidents. If there is great attention paid by managers to punctuality and less to quality, punctuality receives greater emphasis in the eyes of everyone.

The comment about coaching and teaching by leaders indicates the degree of social integration there needs to be between the opinion formers and those holding the opinions and producing the behaviour that those opinions shape. Research on how people learn demonstrates that attitude formation is developed effectively by social interaction and scarcely at all by other methods. Exhortation and written instructions or assurances are likely to do little to change the culture of an organization; working closely with people can, as changing behaviour can lead to a change of attitude.

The most significant reinforcement of attitudes and beliefs comes from that which is tangible and visible. What do people need to do to get a pay rise? What do you have to do to get promoted? What can lead to people being dismissed? Those working in and around organizations usually want the first two and try to avoid the third. If loyalty is rewarded, you will get loyalty but may not get performance. If performance is rewarded, people will at least try to deliver performance.

Organizational culture is the concern of all staff and change in a culture is effective and swift only when there is wide agreement and ownership concerning the change to be sought. Such agreement seems to be best obtained, paradoxically, through a recognition and toleration of a legitimate variety of views and styles on less central matters. Exhortation from an elevated position in a hierarchy, though possibly helpful, is not a guarantee of effectiveness in the pursuit of cultural change.

KEY CONCEPT 19

Culture is hard to change. Those creating a business may be able to build a corporate culture from scratch by personal example, explanation and exhortation. Those aiming to change an existing corporate culture will find it much harder and slower.

In the last chapter we saw that a single undertaking may have several types of structure within it. Culture is similar in that there are varying emphases within a business. All organizations, especially professional organizations, contain groupings each with a distinctive culture, depending on its members' views, the nature of its expertise or tasks, its history and so on. A visitor walking round the premises of any organization notices different cultures in different areas; when this variety is respected, the culture of the organization as a whole will be quite different from that in an organization where such variety is suppressed. Consider these three stereotypical sub-cultures within a single business:

Managerial: Key values are efficiency, profitability, competitiveness, quality and service. Managers look for tight controls, clear structures, and acceptance of authority. They like money, power, status and upward mobility. They dress conventionally and respect analytical ability, planning skills, communication skills and decision-making skills.

Sales and Marketing: Values relate to competitiveness, growth and individual achievement. Less regard than among managers for tight controls and less interest in quantitative analysis. Motivated by money and status, they allow more scope for individuality in dress and behaviour. The skills they respect in particular are communication, negotiation and interpersonal skills.

Scientific and Technical: Values are determined more by a professional reference group than by the employing organization. Money and position in the hierarchy are relatively unimportant compared to the challenge of the job and the sense of freedom and achievement.

Schein's secondary mechanisms for articulating culture are:

a the organizational structure;

b systems and procedures;

c space, buildings and façades;

d stories and legends about important events and people;

e formal statements of philosophy and policy.

This introduces a wider range of possible actions, but we are now considering things that are rather easier. Notice that the formal statement (the attempt to change attitudes) comes at the end. So often we find in practice that attempts to develop aspects of culture actually begin with formal statements of policy, or that cultural inertia is attributed to the lack of such statements. The connection with structure cannot be emphasized enough, as a bureaucratic structure will, for instance, be the biggest single impediment to introducing a corporate culture emphasizing risk taking and personal initiative. The use of space, façades and stories are tangible ways in which the culture can be expressed. The company logo now assumes extraordinary significance in providing a symbol of corporate identity, which everyone can see, understand and share. The stories that go round the grapevine may be those of management incompetence or greed. On the other hand, they may be stories of initiative or dedication to duty. There may be stories only about managers in key positions or there may be stories about how X saved the day by extraordinary initiative and Y got a letter from the overseas visitor who had appreciated a small act of kindness. These are the things which shape culture and managers can influence all of them, for it is the cultural leaders who will make all of these things happen.

Without a central sense of unity, businesses are no more than a collection of people who would rather be somewhere else because they lack effectiveness and conviction in what they are doing. The effective organization has a few central ideals about which there is a high degree of consensus and those ideals are supported and put into operation by simple rules and clear procedures. The organization that depends principally on rules for its cohesion is in the process of decay.

Reference

Schein, EH (1985) *Organizational Culture and Leadership*, Jossey-Bass, San Francisco.

FURTHER READING

Charles O'Reilly, Jennifer Chatman and David Caldwell developed a model based on the belief that cultures can be distinguished by values that are reinforced within organizations. Their Organizational Culture Profile model (OCP) is a self-reporting tool which makes distinctions according to seven categories: innovation, stability, respect for people, outcome orientation, attention to detail, team orientation and aggressiveness. Their work was reported in O'Reilly, C, Chatman, J and Caldwell, D (1991) People and organizational culture, *Academy of Management Journal*, 34 (3), September 1991. Frankly, it is rather heavy going.

Schein, E H (1985) *Organizational Culture and Leadership*, Jossey-Bass, San Francisco. This is a must for the interested reader. He sets out with clarity and verve all most people ever need to understand organizational culture.

Terrence Deal and Allan Kennedy defined organizational culture as 'the way things get done around here', which has a nice straightforward ring. They set out four different types of culture:

Work-hard, play-hard has rapid feedback/reward and low risk. Stress comes from quantity of work rather than uncertainty. High-speed action leads to high-speed recreation. The examples were restaurants, software companies.

Tough-guy macho has rapid feedback/reward and high risk. Stress comes from high risk and potential loss/gain of reward. They focus on the present rather than the longer-term future. Examples were the police and surgeons.

Process has slow feedback/reward and low risk, resulting in low stress, plodding work, comfort and security. Any stress comes from internal politics and poor systems. Bureaucracy and other means of maintaining the status quo develop. Examples are retail banks and insurance companies.

Bet-the-company culture has slow feedback/reward and high risk, leading to stress coming from high risk and delay before knowing if actions have paid off. The long view is taken, with much emphasis on making sure things happen as planned. Examples are aircraft manufacturers and oil companies.

It is worth reading Deal and Kennedy's book: Deal, TE and Kennedy, AA (2000) *Corporate Culture*, Perseus, Cambridge, MA.

Although not referred to in the chapter, the classic study on variations in business cultures across national boundaries is Hofstede, G (2001) *Culture's Consequences*, Sage, Thousand Oaks, CA.

Chapter Six
Communication

Understanding and being understood

In 1979, at the age of 36, Stephen Hawking was appointed Lucasian Professor of Mathematics at the University of Cambridge. After early research on relativity he studied the 'big bang' theory of when the universe originated. In 1988 he published *A Brief History of Time* to explain his understanding. This achieved a huge worldwide sale that was sustained over a number of years. The work of Professor Hawking is all the more remarkable because he has been suffering since his early twenties with the disabling and progressive motor neurone disease. Normal speech is impossible and he can only communicate through a speech synthesizer, using a keyboard.

The example of Stephen Hawking is appropriate to introduce this chapter because of a number of communication features which his story illustrates. First, he had to use a code to understand and to explain the abstruse subject of his analysis. His code was mathematics, the most universal of all explanatory codes. The code sums up and explains the concept, just as a hieroglyph on an ancient Egyptian tomb expresses something in a stylized way. Mathematics is universal because it crosses linguistic boundaries, but its use is limited to a small elite.

To reach a wider audience Hawking had to translate his understanding into a different code: the English language. Initially he used English only to expand on his mathematical codings to his academic peers, but then took the further step of communicating his understanding to a much wider public, who would have no chance of being able to comprehend the mathematics, who found the topic of time and space too bewildering to grasp and probably had little interest in it anyway. Some people believe that *A Brief History of Time* could not have been written in any other language, because only English has the range of vocabulary and the subtlety of nuance needed to translate the obscure into the transparent and interesting. Reaching such a huge audience remains a staggering achievement.

Finally Hawking overcame the barrier of his disability. Being unable to speak, he was still able to produce a masterpiece of communication. Communication is a process of coding and decoding, the importance of being able to send messages that people can understand and respond to, and the need constantly to overcome barriers to communication.

In organizational life there is often no satisfactory alternative to face-to-face conversation, and the substitutes may simply dissatisfy both the senders and the receivers of messages. In highly unionized situations, managers can feel that dealing with employee representatives makes it harder rather than easier for them to get their messages through to employees, while employees often regard the carefully minuted proceedings of the consultative committee as a poor substitute for getting an engineer with a kit of tools to come into the workshop and mend the leaking radiator about which they have been complaining for months.

KEY CONCEPT 20

Communication between people always uses code. Codes can be misinterpreted.

A further contradiction is that we have problems of communication while having a surfeit of information. There is an information explosion, not only in volume but also in ways to convey it. Information is inert. Communication is the understanding by the person or group to which the message is sent.

> In 1799, Napoleon Bonaparte was leading his victorious armies on a campaign in the Middle East when 1,200 Turks were captured at Jaffa. When he was asked what should be done with them, he was seized of a sudden fit of coughing and said, '*Ma sacré toux*' (my damned cough). His chief of staff understood him to say, '*Massacrez tous*' (massacre them all), so all 1,200 were executed.
>
> That may or may not be true, but it demonstrates that communication only works when the receiver gets the right message, understands it correctly and takes the correct action.

The telecommunications analogy

A convenient and well-established way of illustrating how communication works is to compare the human process with the process of telecommunications. Communication begins with some abstract idea or thought in the mind of the person wanting to convey a message. The first step is for the central nervous system of that person to translate the abstractions through the vocal organs into speech patterns or into some form of written or other visual message. If the channel of communication is speech, the patterns of speech travel through the air as sound waves to be received by the ears and conveyed as nervous impulses to the brain of the receiver. In written communications, the message is either manually, mechanically or electronically transferred and is received by the eyes and conveyed again by nervous impulses to the brain. A further possibility is that the message is conveyed by a different visual image, like a flag or symbol. Every minute of the day we convey messages to each other by our body language. If someone blushes with embarrassment, trembles with fear or roars with laughter until the tears roll down their cheeks, they are conveying a clear message, even though it is involuntary. Beckoning, smiling and shaking a fist in anger are visual messages that are deliberate and controlled.

The message, having been transmitted in the code of language or image, is unscrambled in the central nervous system of the receiver, which then enables the listener to understand: the message is received.

Through these various stages of translation from the mind of one to the mind of the other there are a number of points at which error is possible, and even likely. It is almost impossible to know whether the abstract idea in the mind of one person has transferred itself accurately to the mind of the other, so one essential element in the whole process is feedback. This completes the circuit so that there is some indication from the listener that the message has been received and understood. It will also give some indication to the transmitter of the quality of the message that has been received. If the transmitter expects a reaction of pleasure but the feedback is a frown, there is an immediate opportunity to identify the inaccuracy and correct it.

A further element in the communication process is 'noise', used as a generic term to describe anything that interferes in the transmission process: inaudibility, inattention, physical noise and so forth. The degree to which some noise element is present will impair the quality of both transmission and feedback.

Increasing the amount of information can impair rather than improve communication, as information becomes communication only where there is an exchange with the receiver signalling understanding of the correct meaning by feedback to the sender. Information output that is not attuned to the needs of the receiver will obscure rather than clarify the receiver's understanding.

Methods of communication

The method of communication that is used will depend on the nature of the communication that is to take place. A couple commissioning an architect to design a house for them will communicate mainly by speech, face to face, as they struggle to translate their shared vision of the ideal house into a collection of words – the code – that will subsequently be translated into an identical vision in the mind of the architect. The architect will probably provide feedback by making rough sketches or restating what they have said in a slightly different way so that they can confirm how well the vision has been understood. When the house is being built, the builder will work to the architect's drawings. There will be clarification and additional explanation, but the main method of communication will be the drawings with the dimensions of the house and working instructions. When the builder pays an electrician for wiring the house, the payment will be accompanied by a payslip: a written message containing information of great importance to the recipient and rarely accompanied by spoken explanation – clear writing is all that is required.

Within a business there is a great deal of communicating. For the business to function there needs to be a constant flow of information and understanding both with those inside and with those outside. The best method will vary according to its objective. There are various channels through which messages can be transmitted.

The hierarchy or formal arrangement of working relationships is itself a communication as it tells organization members important things about their 'place': how distant they are from the centre and what their official status is. The structure is also a prime communications medium, as there is an assumption that information will travel up, across and down it, enshrined in doctrines of responsibility, accountability and reporting, to say nothing of grievance and disciplinary procedures, which invariably nominate stages in the procedure by identifying them with office holders in the structure. The formal structure also has lateral as well as vertical connections, which are used to provide communication relating to coordination, mutual support and advice. This is the beginning of the networking that is an essential part of the core of management work, as was described earlier.

Behind and between the formal lines is the informal structure or grapevine through which passes information that has not been officially sanctioned. Although not deliberately created, no organizational communication is complete without it. The grapevine has the advantage of being a spontaneous form of expression, providing the satisfaction of talking face to face, and it can often be both more rapid and more informative than official communications. Its operation does not follow the same pattern as the spread of rumours, when the amount of rumoured information increases as the amount of official communication decreases. As the level of official communication goes up there is a fuelling of informal discussion and interpretation of it. Only in extreme cases of information suppression is there enough stimulus to speculation for rumour to grow in order to fill the gaps that the official processes leave.

Informal channels are often used by managers to pass on information that they cannot convey formally, because they are not yet sure of their ground. Also, they may use informal methods to test reaction to a possible move. It is now commonplace for government ministers to test possible reaction to a proposed initiative by 'leaking' some significant details. Press and backbencher reaction then enables them to see difficulties with the initiative that they had not already perceived, so that the eventual formal announcement can be of a modified proposal that is more acceptable and the authority of the minister has not been undermined by being formally associated with an impracticable venture: for some strange reason this is disparaged as a 'U-turn' or 'climb-down' instead of as a constructive response to criticism.

Most of the messages passing through the formal and informal organization structure will be by word of mouth, and we have already seen the preference for this mode of communication demonstrated by research. It is not, of course, only one person speaking with one other. It includes interchange face to face, in small groups and committees, as well as the rarer address to a large meeting.

Written material sometimes stands on its own as a message, so that the monthly statement of pay and statutory deductions is seldom a basis for discussion, unless it is incorrect. Other written material is an adjunct to discussion: the agenda for a meeting, the draft report, the letter confirming an order of material from a supplier '... as discussed with your representative'. It is a form of communication which is used often not to convey information for the first and final time, but as a preliminary to, or confirmation of, some action being discussed. The form can vary from letter to memorandum, from noticeboard to house journal, from job specification to sales order to instruction manual and many more. It is important that it should be used in circumstances for which it is appropriate. Changes in behaviour are seldom likely to follow from written instructions or particulars only. Posters and warning notices have limited effect in persuading employees to adopt safer working practices, for instance, like the stark 'Smoking kills' on cigarette packets.

It is difficult to assess the change brought about by the various electronic means of communication. E-mail has replaced quite a lot of memoranda and some telephone messages. It is quick and easy and there is little embarrassment about spelling mistakes being found out; they are acceptable because of the informality of the medium. As replacements for telephone conversations, they have the attraction that you can say what you want to say without interruption and without social pleasantries or distractions. If a matter needs to be discussed, then video conferencing can be an effective substitute for a face-to-face meeting. It is difficult to see that the amount of word-of-mouth communication will decline.

In November 2011, Thierry Breton, chief executive of the French telecoms business Atos, made the astonishing claim that internal e-mails would be eliminated throughout Atos by 2014. This was astonishing not only because of the nature of the business but also its size, with 80,000 employees in 42 countries offering consulting and technology services to a range of high-profile customers, including Boots, Fiat, Philips, Reuters and the Olympic Games. The reasons were:

a The majority of new graduates joining the business did not use e-mails at all, preferring social networking sites.

b Employees received on average over 100 e-mails a day. They found 15 per cent of the messages useful, and the rest was lost time, but they still read them for fear of missing something.

c Taking account of time spent at home 'catching up', they realized that they were spending 15 to 20 hours a week checking and answering internal e-mails.

There is no doubt that the various new means of instant communication have great benefits, but there are disadvantages as well and talking with people face to face remains the most effective method and is still the most common.

Meetings

Meetings have become the focus of adult interactions and communication within organizations. Although the overt reasons for the meeting may be to make decisions and recommendations, and to analyse and report and deal with information, the covert reasons are often as important for organizational communication. For example:

Cohesion: Physically bringing people together allows them to chat before or after, catch each other's eye, joke, feel part of the whole. Distrust and misunderstanding easily develop between colleagues, especially if they communicate only by impersonal means. Meetings can help greatly in overcoming those problems as well as building the social cohesion of the wider group.

Catharsis: A further social purpose of meetings is the opportunity to get anger out even where nothing can be done about it. A point of view expressed or a sense of frustration made clear is better than either of those being suppressed: at least other people know and understand.

Involvement: The importance attached to participation is an obvious covert reason for holding meetings. There is the axiomatic Key Concept 2 as well as the need to get the maximum input in terms of ideas and shrewd experience.

Learning about both content and process takes place in meetings, but also learning about the culture of the business or section.

Structures for dissent: Disagreement, conflict and dissent are an inevitable part of business life. Meetings can deal with this in different ways: by allowing heated discussion, by suggesting that people report back next time, or by ignoring the dissent.

KEY CONCEPT 21

The method of communication has to be selected according to the nature of the message and the recipients. Simply providing information is not sufficient; it has to be sent in a form that will elicit the desired response.

Barriers to communication

It is the listener, the observer or reader who determines the extent to which the message is understood. What we hear, see or understand is shaped very largely by our own experience and background. We do not hear what people tell us, we hear what our minds tell us they have said, and the two may be different. There are various ways in which expectation determines communication content and these can impair the accuracy of message transmission, acting as 'noise', interfering both with transmission and feedback. We will look at some of the principal difficulties.

The frame of reference. Few of us change our opinions alone, because we are influenced by the group with which we identify ourselves: the reference group. If a particular group of people hold certain values in common, individual members of that group will not easily modify their values unless and until there is a value shift through the group as a whole. This has been shown by the difficulties involved in trying to alert young people to the risks of AIDS and drug abuse. Appeals to the individual, especially alarmist preoccupation with the risk of death, were less effective than working through the common values held by people in the age group.

Whenever a matter is being discussed, the people among whom it is being considered will view it from their particular frame of reference. Where the frames of reference of transmitter and receiver differ widely, there may be substantial difficulties in accurate transmission of messages and even greater difficulties in ensuring that the response of the receiver is that which the transmitter intended.

Stereotyping is an extreme form of letting expectation determine communication content, where we expect a particular type of statement or particular type of attitude from a stereotype of a person. There is a stereotype expectation about the Scots, that they will be mean or at least extremely careful with their money. People also have stereotypes of certain office holders. There is a widespread stereotype of union officials which shows them as being militant, politically extreme in one, and only one, direction, unreasonable, unintelligent and obstructive. Equally, there are widespread stereotypes of different types of manager and for some people there is a stereotype of managers as a whole. One of the greatest difficulties in achieving equal opportunities at work is the challenging of deeply held stereotypes about men and women or those of varied cultural background. There are also stereotypes relating to age, such as an older person being seen as unable to stand the pace, no longer able to think quickly and unwilling to change.

The problem of stereotypes is that we need them as a simple means of organizing our lives. Elderly people living alone are advised not to admit strangers to their house without proper authority. Children are instructed by their parents not to talk to strange men. Not all strangers are dangerous, just as not all older people are unable to stand the pace, but to stereotype a stranger as dangerous to children or to elderly people answering the door is a simple common-sense useful rule of thumb.

The effect of these stereotypes in communication matters is that the person who encounters someone for whom they have a stereotype will begin hearing what the person says in the light of the stereotype held. If somebody has stereotyped pictures in their mind of the Irish and of union officials, and if they then meet a union official with an Irish accent, they will begin hearing what that person says and evaluating it in the context of their expectations. It will be some time before their listening, understanding and evaluation will adjust to the actual performance they are witnessing in contrast to that which they expected.

Cognitive dissonance is the extent to which people will cope successfully with information inputs that they find irreconcilable in some particular way. If someone receives information that is consistent with what they already believe, they are likely to understand it, believe it, remember it and take action upon it. If, however, they receive information that is inconsistent with their established beliefs, they will have genuine difficulty in understanding, remembering and taking action. If people believe in ghosts they will not readily abandon that belief or the behaviour that accompanies it. No matter what convincing arguments are produced, they will require a great deal of persuasion over a long time before they will cheerfully walk through allegedly haunted houses.

That type of problem can be found time and time again in working situations. It has an additional dimension to it. Not only do recipients of information find it difficult to understand, remember and take action, they will also grapple with the dissonance that the problematical new information presents. One of the ways in which they do this is to distort the message so that what they hear is what they want to hear, what they expect to hear and can easily understand rather than the difficult, challenging information that is being put to them.

Halo or horns? is a slightly different aspect of expectation determining communication content, which causes receivers of information to move to extremes of either acceptance or rejection. When we are listening to somebody in whom we have confidence and who has earned our trust we may be predisposed to agree with what they say because we have placed an imaginary halo around their head. Because of our experience of their trustworthiness and reliability we have an expectation that what they say will be trustworthy and reliable. On the other hand, if we have learned to distrust someone, then what we hear them say will be either ignored or treated with considerable caution. A mother might be very reluctant for her child to talk to a strange man in the park, but would positively encourage the child to talk to that same strange man if he were a doctor in his surgery.

Semantics and jargon can cause difficulty as ideas cannot be transferred directly because meaning cannot be transferred; all the communicators can use as their vehicle is words, behaviour or symbols: codes. Unfortunately, the same symbols may suggest different meanings to different people. The meanings are in the hearers rather than the speakers and certainly not in the words themselves. A simple example of this is 'quite ill', which could have a variety of weightings according to how it was heard and the circumstances in which the comment was made.

The problem of jargon is where a word or a phrase has a specialized meaning that is immediately understandable by the experts, but meaningless or misleading to those who do not share the specialized knowledge. In this book there have already been several references to hierarchy. On one occasion an examination answer paper contained the phrase 'high Iraqui'. The unfamiliarity of the word 'hierarchy' had been completely misinterpreted by that particular receiver, who had imposed her own meaning on what she heard because of the need to make sense of what it was that she received. Another interesting example was in a school of motoring, where for many years trainee drivers were given the instruction 'clutch out' or 'clutch in', which nearly always confused the trainee. Later the standard instruction was altered to 'clutch down' or 'clutch up'.

Not paying attention and forgetting is the final combination of problems to consider here. First is the extent to which people do not pay attention to what is being said or to what they see. There is a human predilection to be selective in attention. There are many examples of this, perhaps the most common being the way in which a listener can focus attention on a comment being made by one person in a general babble of sound by a group of people. This is complicated by the problem of noise, which we have already considered, but it has the effect of the listener trying very hard to suppress all signals other than the particular one that they are trying to pick up. Some people believe our ability to maintain concentration (our attention span) is getting steadily shorter.

FURTHER READING

For general reading on communications at work, try Gerson, SJ and Gerson, SM (2007) *Workplace Communication: Process and product*, Pearson Prentice Hall, Upper Saddle River, NJ; Gurak, LJ and Lannon, JM (2012) *Strategies for Technical Communication in the Workplace*, John Wiley & Sons, Inc, Hoboken, NJ.

A print-on-demand title from Jossey-Bass is Perkins, PS (2008) *The Art and Science of Communication: Tools for effective communication in the workplace*, Jossey-Bass, San Francisco.

Two older publications about informal channels are Davis, K (1953) Management communication and the grapevine, *Harvard Business Review*, Sept/Oct, pp 43–49 and Knippen, J (1974) Grapevine communication: management employees, *Journal of Business Research*, January, pp 47–58.

Chapter Seven
Selecting team members

Few managers are able to pick their own team. A manager moving into a new post is the newcomer surrounded by people who are already established. Except in rare circumstances it is unethical, unlawful, too expensive, impractical or simply foolish to discard those who are established and replace them with one's own nominees. Selecting team members is, therefore, a quite different activity for the individual manager than it is for HR people, who are recruiting people for the organization as a whole.

HR have to consider the broad issues such as equality of opportunity, promotion prospects, pension entitlement and the degree to which the potential recruit is likely to 'fit' the corporate culture. In contrast, the individual manager is an occasional selector only, and is concerned much more with the internal dynamics of the working team and the nature of the working relationship with the person appointed. All concerned in the selection decision – HR, individual manager and potential recruit – aim for a good match between people appointed and the situation in which they will be working, but each has a different perspective. This chapter is about the decision making of the individual manager trying to develop and maintain a balanced working team.

The manager selects a few members of the team either single-handed or in consultation with others, but tolerates the vagaries of many others. One could almost say that picking one's own people is an abdication of management, a part of the art being to organize and coordinate the contribution of different types of people, including those one does not get on with.

KEY CONCEPT 22

In selecting people for your team, make sure you pick the right people, not just those you like.

The employment contract

Selecting people for jobs is a process of setting up an employment contract between the individual employee and the employing organization. This is much more than the legally binding contract of employment which summarizes the rights and obligations of the two parties; it is matching two sets of needs and expectations. I use the term 'employing organization' rather than 'employer' in this context because it is that situation which is the arena within which both sets of expectation will be met, or not. It is natural to think in terms of what contribution to business success will be made by the employee, although this is seldom thought out very clearly and often centres round narrow, personal preferences of the manager in charge of the section. It is also accepted that individual employees expect certain satisfactions from their employment, but frequently these two sets of requirements are seen as being satisfied independently of each other: the employee gets a salary, some holiday and contributions to a pension scheme in exchange for which personal interest and achievement are set aside in order to accommodate the routine requirements of the employer. Satisfactions for either party are likely to be mainly at the expense of the other. In reaction against this, there are some employment situations where too much is done to satisfy the employee, so that the attempt is self-defeating. The conditions of work are enhanced with more money, longer holidays, free meals, flexible working hours or other treats, but nothing is done about the work, which remains an irksome necessity to be tolerated with as much restraint and dignity as possible. The result is often inefficiency, slackness and employees who not only are dissatisfied with their work, but also feel guilty about their dissatisfaction with the cornucopia of good conditions that surrounds them.

The essence of the employment contract idea is simply that the two sets of needs are not independent but complementary; the employee seeks satisfaction in the work done as well as from the circumstances in which it is done, and employees satisfied with their work will be more secure, more creative, more responsive to customers, more reliable and more efficient. HR can do no more than clear away some of the possible impediments to a good employment contract. It is the individual manager who clarifies the needs of the organization and integrates those with the needs of the employee, so that both are satisfied by the same processes.

KEY CONCEPT 23

Selection matches the needs of the business with those of the recruit; many of these needs are the same.

The importance of this approach is that the manager has to think just as much about what the appointee is looking for as about what the job requirements are. Both selector and appointee are choosing and it is important to both that each makes a sound decision.

Attracting team members

People, working groups and departments acquire reputations and one aspect of those reputations is to influence the number and type of people who want to join the group. All managers are interested in the reputation that they and their departments enjoy. 'A really first-class, very enthusiastic bunch of people' is the sort of label that is likely to attract people seeking that sort of working environment, whereas 'It is very well run and the manager is scrupulously fair' conveys a different image that will appeal to different people.

Reputations can be reliable indicators within an organization, where the grapevine will do its work, but are much less useful as indicators to those outside, who may be influenced more by stereotypes. One local government official grumbled to me about the difficulty of recruiting people other than those who were looking for 'a safe billet'. She felt that local government had a popular image of being comfortable but dull and that this image became a self-fulfilling prophecy, as applicants came either because that was what they wanted or because they could not find anything else and thought themselves into the model they expected.

The reputation of the employing organization in the labour markets is mainly a job for HR, but other managers can ensure that they are people worth working with and their departments worth working in. They can, however, do little to alter the truth. So they need to declare and embody what they actually are and how they really work, rather than generate some artificial picture of what they think will make them attractive. Managers are attracting potential team members in two ways. First, they are attracting the person who is looking for an internal move or awaiting their new posting. In this context, reputation can be vitally important. If there is a loosely structured method of career advance, wherein individuals apply for jobs that appeal to them, managers are traders on the internal labour market and will want to create a climate of opinion about who would fit into their department before specific vacancies occur. If movement is centrally controlled, so that individuals are moved between jobs, then the reputation of an individual manager or department will affect the attitude and expectations of the new arrival.

Secondly, managers are attracting potential members by creating recommendations. Existing employees ask if there may be a vacancy for their next-door neighbour, cousin, son, or someone with whom they have worked previously. This remains a popular way in which new employees are attracted, but not necessarily selected. It is also the way in which organizations perpetuate the existing make-up of the workforce because new recruits tend to be similar to those who recommend them. This can stultify the development of a group of employees with contrasted abilities and perspectives, as well as perhaps denying employment opportunities to certain social groups. The reputation of candidates and of departments and organizations in which candidates seek openings spreads informally.

Application forms are nearly always available for scrutiny. Either the candidate is from outside and is completing one with the vacancy in view, or is an insider who completed a form some time previously. The value of this document is that it sets out systematically the basic information about the person being considered. Because of this orderly display, it is also the common basis for the selection interview. Surveying application forms from candidates enables one quickly to pick up and compare a few key points about a number of applicants, such as age, qualifications, current post, salary and location. It is the easiest and most effective method of producing a short list. The way in which information about candidates is displayed in it provides a logical sequence for the selection interview. The information is presented in biographical sequence so as to provide a pattern for questioning that is fruitful for the interviewer and coherent to the respondent. Some forms also provide space by each entry for the interviewers to make their own comments.

Curricula vitae. A long-standing practice, now becoming more widespread, is for candidates to submit a curriculum vitae (CV). This is often attractive to those who are articulate and experienced, as it enables them to tell their story in their own way, with the degree of detail and emphasis which gives the most positive picture of their track record and potential. It can appeal to recruiters as well because the style and approach of the CV give a number of individual clues about the candidate which are obscured by the standardized method of the application form. The shortcomings of the CV are that systematic comparison is difficult and judgements are likely to be based on the more intangible aspects of the application, and on the style rather than substance of the candidate. The CV writer necessarily uses a broad approach, making every possible point in a very general way rather than tailoring the information to the vacancy. Also, a CV will emphasize the positive, while the application form may ask for information that the candidate tries to avoid or gloss over.

Letters. Another tactic is to ask candidates to fill in a form but also to write a letter of application, with the form setting out the biographical information systematically and the letter making the case for that particular person fitting the specific vacancy. This requires clear advice to candidates on what the letter should contain; otherwise the letter may simply restate what is in the form with varying levels of self-consciousness.

Job descriptions. Descriptions of the post may be available in detailed documents, or simply be a picture in the mind of the selector. Usually the written job description is preferred, as it sets out what candidates want to know about the job for which they are applying, and summarizes for selectors the points against which they are matching those interviewed. It is also argued that the process of producing the job description clarifies for the selector the details of the job to be done.

Candidate specifications. Profiles of the ideal candidate, prepared beforehand on the basis of the job description, may also be available. This too may be just a picture in the mind of the selector, or it may be a written profile that specifies requirements in terms of qualifications, length and type of working experience, aptitudes, skills and intelligence. The advantage of this is mainly in the short-listing of candidates, comparing application form details with points in the specification. It then has a later role in the examination of the ways in which preferred candidates do not quite meet the specification and deciding which requirements are the most important. The possible hazard is the word 'ideal', which some people writing specifications may choose to interpret as 'perfect' or even 'my brother-in-law'. Perfect candidates are very hard indeed to find. Realism is required.

Candidate specification and job description are generic terms to cover the two types of document which are fundamental to the recruitment and selection process, but clever people are regularly thinking up new terms, such as role profile, task definition, competency framework, requisite skill set, personnel outline and person specification. What matters is to start with what the person will have to do and then to set out what a candidate has to be and able to do to meet those requirements.

KEY CONCEPT 24

The requirements of the job must be thoroughly clear before the type of candidate is specified.

Test scores are sometimes available in larger organizations, or where external candidates are being put forward for consideration by consultants. Easiest to deal with is a test of skill or proficiency, such as a typing or driving test, which indicates a level of competence by a generally acknowledged yardstick. Tests of intelligence (often cloaked by some euphemism) are not so easy to use. They measure some of a person's abilities against a standardized indicator, such as intelligence quotient or quartiles of the general population, but there is often resistance from candidates to taking such tests, especially if they are well established in their careers and feel that undertaking such tests is like testing Giotto to see if he knows how to hold a paint brush. A test of this type that is widely used is the Graduate Management Admission Test, which is administered by the University of Princeton and used by business schools in many countries to decide whether or not candidates will be able to cope with their master's programmes. More specialized are tests of aptitude, like those used to select prospective trainees for aircrew duties or recruits for engineering apprenticeships. They assess not skill but the potential to develop a skill that depends on some aspect of natural aptitude like manual dexterity or spatial judgement.

Potential recruits to the fire services, for instance, are tested for their ability to deal with heights and to deal with confined spaces, as well as their physical stamina.

The most controversial tests are those of personality, which claim to produce profiles of human traits and motivation, so that selectors can have a prediction about a candidate's potential for a post that goes beyond an assessment of existing skills, intelligence and aptitudes. Some authorities question this type of testing on the basis that personality cannot be measured and others because of contrasting views on how personality is constructed. This is especially difficult because of a bias within tests towards some cultural norms but not others.

References provided by previous employers, family friends and Justices of the Peace are notoriously unhelpful and often misleading, but they are still extensively used. They are supposed to provide evidence of character, but the self-selecting nature of their nomination by candidates makes their objectivity questionable. Candidates choose reference writers because they think they will provide a 'good' reference, and 'bad' references are extremely rare. There appears to be a set of coded messages conveyed by the concluding sentence of reference letters, which will usually be one of the following:

> 'I am delighted to commend Bloggins to you without any reservation...'.
>
> 'I strongly recommend Bloggins as a very well qualified candidate for the vacancy.'
>
> 'I recommend Bloggins to you for serious consideration.'

Any regular attender at selection panels where references are being considered will notice the tendency for battle-weary members of the panel to look at the end of the reference first. If the remainder is read at all, it is interpreted in the light of that key, closing sentence. References may give an insight into the character of the person writing them, but they tell you little about the person on whose behalf the letter has been written. Occasionally candidates are damned, but seldom explicitly, as reference writers seem unwilling to put in writing their reasons for saying that Bloggins is awful. Rare, but potent, is for a referee to decline the invitation to write a reference at all. More common is for the written reference to add an invitation to discuss the matter further by telephone.

Other methods of selection in current use include biodata analysis, which is a systematic examination of the life history of the applicant and scoring certain key points to produce a profile of likely candidates. Larger companies increasingly use assessment centres, whereby a number of short-listed candidates undergo a range of selection methods, including group exercises. This has the value that a variety of evidence is collected and a balanced assessment is reached.

The selection interview

Every time someone is selected to join a team an interview will precede the appointment. Although this is mainly for selector(s) to decide whether the candidate is suitable, candidates will also be making up their minds whether the move is one that they wish to make or not. Some selection processes unreasonably try to rule out the possibility of the candidate deciding against the job as a result of the interview by asking them to declare at the beginning of the interview that they are firm applicants.

The selection interview is partly an initiation rite and the importance of ritual in the selection process should never be underestimated. Candidates arrive in their best clothes and are expected to show deference to the interviewers and great keenness to be employed, while the selectors are unlikely to wear their best clothes, sometimes demonstrate their superiority by being late or preoccupied with other things, and will rarely show enthusiasm to employ the candidate. Although these ritual elements are inevitable in the selection situation, the purpose of the interview goes much further and has as its main objective the ability of the selector to decide whether the candidate is appropriate or inappropriate for the post under consideration. How can this be done effectively?

The interview setting

This should be appropriate for a private conversation, so that the exchanges will be frank and constructive. Many people also feel that the setting should reduce the status barriers between interviewer and applicant on the grounds that the interviewer is in the socially superior position of having a job to offer, or not, while the respondent is in the inferior position of wanting the job and being disposed to propitiate the interviewer in order to get it. If the seating arrangements underplay that distinction, candidates will be more relaxed and more open in what they say. This can be done by avoiding direct, face-to-face interviewing across a desk and moving to a situation where both participants are sitting at the same height, not directly opposed and without any obvious advantage to the interviewer. There is a danger in the setting becoming too informal and thus destroying rather than mitigating the ritual elements. The friendly chat over a drink in a local pub may be pleasantly relaxed and the candidate will probably (eventually) become very loquacious, but it is a difficult 'interview' to structure and may disconcert the candidate, who is expecting something more businesslike.

KEY CONCEPT 25

The selection interview should be an exchange of information, not a battle of wits.

The plan of the interview

This is most easily taken from the sequence of the application form particulars. The development of the questioning then builds logically in the mind of the selector and can be followed constructively by candidates, who can see how the interview is progressing, rather than feeling that there is some hidden agenda that they do not understand and which consequently worries them. There is one preliminary: setting up rapport. At the opening of the interview, candidate and selector assess each other and tune in to each other. It is usually done by exchanging words about trivia (some people believe that it rains frequently in Britain simply to provide a topic of conversation at the opening of interviews), explaining procedure and plenty of nods and smiles. It also gives the selector an opportunity to sketch out what is to happen and where the interview fits in with the rest of the decision-making process.

After the pleasantries, there is a change of pace as the interview moves to information exchange, and we need to remember that the information is moving both ways, not only towards the selector. Candidates from inside the organization will know most of the things they need to make up their minds about the post and will probably have just one or two check questions as well as a keen interest in the type of person the selector is and the people with whom they will be working. The external candidate will have more gaps in understanding to fill in; again the interview is the opportunity. Convention says, however, that candidates do not ask selectors questions about *their* qualifications and ambitions, so they rely on clues and information conveyed unwittingly by interviewers.

The selector has the advantage of being able to structure the encounter, as candidates expect to have to respond to initiatives, rather than take initiatives themselves. The first question is important in setting both the tone and direction of the exchange. Consider this very common opening question: 'Tell me, why have you applied for this job?'

Despite its extensive use, it is an ineffective way to begin, as it puts the candidate on the defensive, feeling the need to say the right thing, whether it is true or not. It is a difficult question to answer, as the reasons for seeking a move are probably varied and hard to summarize. Also, some of the common reasons – more money, dislike of present boss, easier travel, more holidays, more security – are the sort of reasons that candidates often feel inappropriate to mention, especially at the beginning, so they speak vaguely about challenge and unfulfilled potential. The interview thus gets under way as a form of verbal fencing, with the candidate wary of the next question. Now consider this, alternative, opening question: 'Could you give me a general outline of your present responsibilities?'

This has a number of advantages. First, the candidate will know the answer and that answer will be full of relevant, valuable information as it relates to what the candidate can do rather than to any subjective evaluation of motives. Second, it is not likely to be regarded with suspicion by the candidate trying to guess what the question is 'really after'. Third, it will provide an admirable starting point as there will be a number of aspects that could usefully be developed further. This is not to suggest that all selection interviews should start with this particular question, but questions about real facts and events are more sensible and useful than questions that require candidates to speculate or which make them uneasy.

A further development on the interview plan is to take a step back in time to an earlier point in the candidate's career and then move forward to the present, reviewing various developments on the way. This should be done with no more than one backwards move, if possible, as it is much easier to follow something that is explained as it developed rather than in reverse. Selectors get quite bewildered and candidates become incoherent when asked to explain their choice of degree, then their choice of A levels, and then their GCSE performance.

Selectors may find it useful to note key issues and check points. Key issues will be two or three features of information from the application form that stand out as needing clarification or elaboration. A particular episode of previous employment may need to be explored to see the range of responsibilities held, the difficulty of the circumstances or the number of subordinates. There may be key issues in the educational record, overseas experience or work in a specific industry that needs to be discussed. Check points are details that need to be confirmed, like grades in an examination or dates of appointment. All of this has to be done in a framework and atmosphere that is not a sceptical cross-examination of an evasive witness, but a meeting in which the candidates are enabled (not just allowed) to talk about themselves fully, frankly and with relevance to the vacant post. As long as the selector organizes and leads the interview, the information flow from the candidate will be much more useful and informative than if the candidate is required only to provide clipped replies to a list of predetermined questions.

The job of deciding who should be offered the appointment is simple to describe, but less easy to accomplish. It involves deciding first whether there is a good match between the person being considered and the job that has to be done, and second whether there is a good match between the group of people among whom the work will be done and the person being considered.

The first of these decisions is the more straightforward and can be based on the systematic matching by the selector of the job description and candidate specification on the one hand and the information obtained about the candidate on the other. A systematic approach on the basis of good documentation should decide whether someone is appointable or not. Deciding whether or not the candidate would fit socially is more problematic as it raises all the risks of appointing only clones, and the risk of being unlawfully discriminatory. There may be helpful advice from HR if they have run personality tests, but the likelihood of a good match between the prospective new recruit and the other members of the working team is mainly a matter for the selector's judgement.

Consultation with team members can help. The more people who meet the candidate, the more opinions there will be about suitability and the greater willingness to make the match effective, even if individual opinions have been overruled. Information to the candidates can also help. The more frankly they have had problems and opportunities discussed with them, the more prepared they are to make their contribution to a constructive working relationship. Finally, a group of people working together apathetically, poorly organized and critical of their leaders, can undermine the effectiveness of even the most enthusiastic new recruit. A robust, well-organized team of confident people working well together will be able to assimilate some inappropriate appointees without serious trouble. Whereabouts in that spectrum does your team stand?

Whether new team members come from outside the organization or from within, the first few days and weeks are an important period of 'reciprocal moulding' as they are fitted into the structure and into the formal framework of relationships. Wise selections are made to work by sensible induction and even unwise selections can be made tolerable by hard work in the early stages of the working relationship.

FURTHER READING

Little new and thorough work has been published on selection in recent years, but an exception is Breaugh, JA (2009) Employee selection at the beginning of the twenty-first century, *Human Resource Management Review*, **19** (3), September, pp 168–169. This is a review of recent research on areas such as the effect of legal regulation, international and cultural issues, and speculation that the emphasis may be moving away from concentrating on job-relatedness; really for the HR specialist.
The classic work is Smith, MJ and Robertson, IT (1986) *Theory and Practice of Staff Selection*, Macmillan, London. A different approach is Cook, M (2009) *Personnel Selection: Adding value through people*, Wiley-Blackwell, Oxford.
Job descriptions and candidate specifications are the product of job analysis, extensively described in many books about organizational psychology and personnel management. Pearn, M and Kandola, R (1988) *Job Analysis: A practical guide for managers,* Institute of Personnel Management, London, provides an excellent review.

Chapter Eight
Discipline and grievance

Sorting things out when they go wrong

Grievance and discipline are technical terms to describe how to put right a breakdown of mutual confidence between employer and employee, or between managers and managed. There are mutual expectations from the working relationship: the contract. Employees expect, for instance, a congenial working situation with like-minded colleagues, opportunities to use existing skills and to acquire others, work that does not offend their personal value system, acceptable leadership and management from those more senior, and opportunities to grow. Employers will have expectations such as willing participation in the team, conscientious and imaginative use of existing skills and an ability to acquire others, compliance with reasonable instructions from those placed in authority and a willingness to be flexible and accept change.

If something goes wrong so that the employee is dissatisfied, there is potentially a grievance. If the employer is dissatisfied, there is the potential for a disciplinary situation. How do you find ways of avoiding the ultimate sanction of the employee quitting or being dismissed, but at the same time preparing the ground for those sanctions if all else fails?

KEY CONCEPT 26

Grievance and discipline are ways of resolving difficulties in the employment relationship. They are not about punishment or grumbling.

Exercising authority is impersonalized by the use of roles. Everyone in a business has a role. The canteen assistant who tells you that the steak and kidney pudding is off is more believable than the chief executive conveying the same message. Hierarchy confirms the roles and we are predisposed to obey those who outrank us in any hierarchy.

A famous experiment by Stanley Milgram in 1974, with results that were confirmed in a bizarre way in 2010, showed that when people enter a hierarchical system they see themselves acting as agents for carrying out the wishes of someone else. This is the opposite of autonomy when individuals see themselves as acting on their own. There are five bases for this.

a *Parental regulation* inculcates a respect for adult authority in childhood. Parents give a relentless stream of instructions about food, washing, sitting down in a particular place at a particular time, keeping still while your shoes are put on and so on. You feel there is no alternative and you realize that obeying often pays off: there are rewards. Children emerge from the family into the institution of the school and learn how to function in an organization. They are regulated by teachers, but can see that the head teacher in turn regulates the teachers. Throughout this period they are in a subordinate position. Before long they begin to challenge parental authority, but the behaviour of doing as you're told has begun to consolidate. When, as adults, they go to work it may be found that a certain level of dissent is allowable, but the overall situation is one in which they are to do a job prescribed by someone else.

b *Compliance with authority is generally rewarded,* while disobedience is frequently punished. Most significantly, promotion within the hierarchy not only rewards the individual but also ensures the continuity of the hierarchy.

c *Authority is supported by norms of behaviour:* any organization ordinarily has a socially controlling figure. Also, the authority of the controlling figure is limited to the situation. The usher in a cinema wields authority, which vanishes on leaving the premises. Where authority is expected it does not have to be asserted, merely presented.

d *The adult not only takes the voluntary step of deciding which authority system to join but also defines which authority is relevant to which event.* The firefighter may expect instant obedience when calling for everybody to evacuate the building, but not if asking employees to use a different accounting system.

e *The legitimacy of the situation relates to a justifying ideology.* Most employment is in an activity regarded as legitimate, justified by the values and needs of society. This is vital if individuals are to provide willing obedience, as it enables them to see their behaviour as serving a desirable end.

Managers have a framework of organizational justice to ensure obedience. Because individual employees feel their relative weakness in the hierarchy, they seek complementary frameworks to challenge the otherwise unfettered use of managerial disciplinary power: they may join trade unions, but they will always need channels to present their grievances.

KEY CONCEPT 27

People at work are predisposed to obey those in a role that gives them a defined authority.

Both discipline and grievance depend on the procedural framework of *organizational justice*. You may say that this all rather rigid and that there is a preference for more flexible, personal ways of working than procedure offers. Well, hierarchical relationships continue, although deference is in decline. We still seek out the person 'in authority' when we have a grievance and managers readily refer problems they cannot resolve to someone else with a more appropriate role. Procedures may be rigid and mechanical, but they are reliable and we use them even if we do not like them.

What do we mean by discipline?

Discipline is regulating human activity to produce a controlled performance. It ranges from the guard's control of a rabble to accomplishment by lone individuals producing spectacular performance through self-discipline in the control of their own talents and resources. Here is a small hierarchy to explain the different types of discipline:

In *managerial discipline* everything depends on the leader. There is a group of people who are answerable to someone who directs what they should all do. Only through individual direction can that group of people produce a worthwhile performance, like the conductor of an orchestra.

Team discipline is where the quality of the performance depends on the mutual dependence of all, and that mutual dependence derives from a commitment by each member to the total enterprise: the failure of one would be the downfall of all. This is usually found in relatively small working groups, like a sports team or an autonomous working group in a factory.

Self-discipline is like that of the juggler or the skilled artisan, where a solo performer is absolutely dependent on training, expertise and self-control.

Discipline can be a valuable quality for the individual who is subject to it, although the form of discipline depends not only on the individual employee but also on the task and the way it is organized. The development of self-discipline is easier in some jobs than others and many of the job redesign initiatives of recent years have been directed at providing scope for job holders to exercise self-discipline and find a degree of autonomy from managerial discipline. However, even the most accomplished solo performer has at some time been dependent on others for training and advice, and every team has its coach.

Managers are not dealing with discipline only when rebuking latecomers or warning people of possible dismissal. They are developing the coordinated discipline of the working team, engendering that *esprit de corps* which makes the whole greater than the sum of the parts. They are training the new recruit who must not let down the rest, puzzling over why A is fitting in well while B is still struggling. Managers are also providing people with the means to develop the self-discipline that will give them autonomy, responsibility and the capacity to maximize their powers. The independence and autonomy that self-discipline produces also bring the greatest degree of personal satisfaction, and often the largest pay packet. Furthermore, the movement between the three forms of discipline represents a declining degree of managerial involvement.

What do we mean by grievance?

It is useful to distinguish between the terms dissatisfaction, complaint and grievance as follows: dissatisfaction is anything that disturbs an employee, whether or not it is expressed in words, complaint is dissatisfaction brought to the attention of a manager or other responsible person and grievance is a complaint that has been formally presented to an appropriate management representative, thereby invoking procedure. Grievance is a formal, relatively drastic step, compared with simply complaining.

It is much more important for management to know about dissatisfaction. Although nothing is being expressed, the feeling of hurt following failure to get a pay rise or the frustration about shortage of materials can quickly influence performance. Much dissatisfaction never turns into complaint, as something happens to make it unnecessary. Dissatisfaction evaporates with a night's sleep, after a cup of coffee with a colleague, or when the cause of the dissatisfaction is in some other way removed. The few dissatisfactions that do produce complaint are also most likely to resolve themselves at that stage. The person hearing the complaint explains things in a way that the dissatisfied employee had not previously appreciated, or takes action to get at the root of the problem.

Grievances are rare since few employees will openly question their superior's judgement, whatever their private opinion may be, and fewer still will risk being stigmatized as a troublemaker. Also, some people do not initiate grievances because they believe that nothing will be done. The dissatisfaction lying beneath a repressed grievance can produce all manner of unsatisfactory work behaviours, from apathy to arson. Individual dissatisfaction can lead to the loss of a potentially valuable employee; collective dissatisfaction can lead to industrial action. The challenge for managers is to nose out dissatisfaction, give it 24 hours to heal itself (like the good night's sleep), see if it has survived the 24 hours and then try to resolve it; this is management at its most skilful.

In dealing with complaints it is important to determine what lies behind the complaint as well as the complaint being expressed; not only verifying the facts, which are the *manifest* content of the complaint, but also determining the feelings behind the facts: the *latent* content. An employee who complains of the supervisor being a bully may actually be expressing something rather different, such as the employee's attitude to any authority figure, not simply the supervisor who was the subject of the complaint.

KEY CONCEPT 28

A complaint is an opportunity for a manager to manage. A grievance is the outcome of a manager not being able to manage.

The business requires a framework of justice to surround the employment relationship so that managers and supervisors, as well as other employees, know where they stand when dissatisfaction develops. The first part of this is culture.

The *culture* of an organization affects the behaviour of people within it and develops norms that are hard to alter and which provide a pattern of conformity. If, for instance, everyone is in the habit of arriving 10 minutes late, a 'new broom' manager will have a struggle to change the habit. If everyone is in the habit of arriving punctually, a new recruit who often arrives late will come under strong social pressure to conform, without need for recourse to management action. Culture also affects the freedom and candour with which people discuss dissatisfactions with their managers without allowing them to fester.

Every workplace has *rules*; the difficulty is to have rules that people will honour. Some rules come from legislation, such as the tachograph requirement for HGV drivers, but most are tailored to meet the particular requirements of the organization in which they apply. For example, rules about personal cleanliness are essential in a food factory but less stringent in a garage.

Rules should be clear and readily understood; the number should be sufficient to cover all obvious and usual disciplinary matters. To ensure general compliance it is helpful if rules are jointly determined, but it is more common for management to formulate the rules and for employee representatives eventually to concur with them. Rules can be roughly grouped into various types: (a) Negligence is failure to do the job properly and is different from incompetence. An incompetent person cannot do the job; a negligent person can do the job but hasn't.

(b) Unreliability is failure to attend work as required, being either late or absent. (c) Insubordination is refusal to obey an instruction, or deliberate disrespect to someone in a position of authority. It is not to be confused with the use of bad language. Some of the most entertaining cases in employment tribunals have involved weighty consideration of whether or not colourful language was intended to be insubordinate. (d) Failure to respect the rights of others covers a range of behaviours that are unlawful or socially unacceptable. Fighting is clearly identifiable, but harassment or intimidation may be more difficult to establish. (e) Theft is another clear-cut aspect of behaviour that is unacceptable when it is from another employee, but theft from the business should be supported by very explicit rules, as stealing company property is regarded by many offenders as one of the perks of the job. How often have you taken home a box of paper clips or a felt-tip pen without any thought that you were stealing from the employer? (f) Safety offences are those aspects of behaviour that can cause a hazard.

The value of rules is to provide guidelines on what people should do, as the majority will comply. It is difficult to apply rules that do not command general acceptance.

Procedural sequence is the clear, unvarying logic of procedure, which should be well known and trusted. Procedure makes clear, for example, who does and who does not have the power to dismiss. The dissatisfied employee, who is wondering whether or not to turn a complaint into a formal grievance, knows who will hear the grievance and where an appeal could be lodged. This security of procedure, where step B always follows step A, is needed by managers as well as by employees, as it provides them with their authority as well as limiting the scope of their actions.

Managerial self-discipline preserves general respect for the justice framework by managers exercising self-discipline in how they work within it. With very good intentions, some senior managers maintain an 'open door' policy with the message: 'My door is always open … call in any time you feel I can help you'. This has advantages, but it has drawbacks if it encourages people to bypass middle managers, undermining the authority of role that should be theirs. There is also the danger that employees come to see settlement of their grievances depending on the personal goodwill of an individual rather than on the business logic or their human and employment rights. ⁻

Managers must be consistent in handling discipline and grievance issues. Whatever the rules are, they will be generally supported only as long as they deserve support. If they are enforced inconsistently they will soon lose any moral authority, and will be obeyed only because of employees' fear of penalties. Equally, the manager who handles grievances quickly and consistently will enjoy the support of a committed group of employees.

The other need for managerial self-discipline is to test the validity of the discipline assumption. Is it a case for disciplinary action or for some other remedy? There is little purpose in suspending someone for negligence when the real problem is lack of training. Many disciplinary problems disappear under analysis, and it is sensible to carry out the analysis before making a possibly unjustified allegation of indiscipline.

Are discipline and grievance procedures equitable?

Well, they won't work well if they're not! They must command support, and they will only command support if they are seen as equitable, truly just and fair. At first it may seem that concern for the individual employee is paramount, but the individual cannot be isolated from everyone else. Fairness should therefore be linked to the interests that all employees have in common in the business, and to the managers who must also perceive the system as equitable if they are to abide by its outcomes.

Procedures have a potential to be fair in that they are *certain*. The conduct of employee relations becomes less haphazard and irrational: people 'know where they stand'. The existence of a rule cannot be denied and opportunities for one party to manipulate and change a rule are reduced. Procedures also have the advantage that they can be *communicated*. Formalizing a procedure that previously existed only in custom and practice clarifies any ambiguities and inconsistencies and compels each party to recognize the role and responsibility of the other. By providing pre-established *avenues for responses* to various contingencies, procedures make it possible for the response to be less random and so fairer. The *impersonal* nature of procedures offers the possibility of removing hostility from the workplace, since an artificial social situation is created in which the ritual displays of aggression towards management are not seen as personal attacks on managers.

The achievement of equity may not match the potential. Procedures cannot impart equity to situations that are basically unfair. It is also impossible through a grievance procedure to overcome accepted norms of inequity in a company, such as greater punctuality being required of manual employees than of white-collar employees.

A further feature of procedural equity is its *similarity to the judicial process*. All procedures adopt certain legalistic mechanisms, such as the right of individuals to be represented and to hear the case against them, but other aspects, such as burdens of proof and strict adherence to precedent, may cause the application of standard remedies rather than the consideration of individual circumstances.

It is a nice irony that *equity is best achieved when procedures are not used*. Procedure is there in the background and expresses principles for fair and effective management of situations. All the time that the principles are followed and the framework for organizational justice is observed, procedure is not invoked; individuals, whether employees or managers, are not named and shamed so that matters are much easier to deal with. Only when the matter is dealt with badly does the procedural step come closer.

The existence of the procedure becomes the incentive rather than the means for action to be taken; it is not an excuse for inaction. Some employment situations require naming and shaming first, with possible remedial action following. In most sports there is on-the-spot penalizing of players for breaking the rules.

The 'red-hot stove' rule of discipline offers the touching of a red-hot stove as an analogy for effective disciplinary action:

1 The burn is immediate. There is no question of cause and effect.

2 You had warning. If the stove was red-hot, you knew what would happen if you touched it.

3 The discipline is consistent. Everyone who touches the stove is burnt.

4 The discipline is impersonal. People are burnt not because of who they are, but because they touch the stove.

The procedural approach can exploit standards of certainty and consistency, which are widely accepted as elements of justice. The extent to which a procedure can do this will depend on the suitability of its structure to local circumstances, the commitment of those who operate it and the way in which it reconciles legalistic and bargaining elements. Procedure is bureaucracy at its best; procedure that is mishandled can become bureaucracy at its worst.

Reference

Milgram, S (1974) *Obedience to Authority*, Tavistock, London.

FURTHER READING

For a more detailed exploration of grievance and discipline at work try Torrington, DP, Hall, LA, Taylor, S and Atkinson, CM (2011) *Human Resource Management*, 8th edn, Pearson Education, Harlow.

Milgram's experiments involved the highly controversial method of giving volunteers the task of delivering electric shocks to someone else without telling them that the shocks were fake. It makes fascinating reading in Milgram, S (1974) *Obedience to Authority*, Tavistock, London, and in Milgram, S (1992) *The Individual in a Social World*, 2nd edn, Harper & Row, New York. There is an even more alarming follow-up described by Nick, C and Eltchaninoff, M (2010) *L'Expérience Extrême*, Don Quichotte, Paris. Do you think Milgram's experiments would have had a different outcome if the subjects had included women as well as men?

Three recent publications set out the current legal situation in Britain about grievance and discipline, taking slightly different perspectives: ACAS (2009) *Disciplinary and grievance procedures*. Code of Practice 1, Advisory, Conciliation and Advisory Service, London; BIS (2009) *Avoiding and resolving discipline and grievance issues at work*, Department for Business Innovation and Skills, London; CIPD (2009) *Discipline and grievances at work*, Chartered Institute of Personnel and Development, London.

Chapter Nine
Training

How people learn and how to teach them

Managers often have to act as teachers. Methods of teaching vary according to what in the learner is being developed. Learning to use a keyboard requires a different method from that for understanding how to use a new computer program, and how to sell the system to customers requires another. In this chapter I'm going to describe learning in groups and then make some comments about continuous learning.

KEY CONCEPT 29

Teaching people requires an approach appropriate to what in the learner is to be developed: practical skill or drill, understanding something more complex, learning how to work with other people.

Learning in groups

Acquiring any type of social skill, like selling or negotiation or presentation or customer care, is enabling people to develop the capacity to alter their attitudes and social behaviours. Much of contemporary customer care training has this as its basis. The theory is that dealing with customers requires people to be confident of their own ability to deal with others, losing feelings of insecurity and discovering how they are able to elicit a positive response.

Members of a learning group both compete and cooperate. They will cooperate in the shared task of seeking understanding and developing answers, but they will also compete in wanting to appear shrewd, fluent and perceptive, especially if there are inequalities of status in the group. They will be even more anxious not to appear foolish. Members of the group will look to the leader for structure at the beginning: a strong indication of how to get started and assistance in developing the social interaction of the group process. As discussion unfolds, the teacher will become less obviously necessary to the group, but will still need to control the exchanges to ensure their effectiveness. This later control is the hardest part, as the voluble need to be reigned in frequently and the diffident encouraged.

Small informal groups are used extensively in business life, especially since the introduction of team briefing, quality circles and other attempts at employee involvement. It is now quite common to see a group of a dozen people standing in a circle at the entrance to a supermarket, having a meeting. This is usually near the beginning of a normal working shift and it brings together section managers or other representatives to exchange information which has to be shared. This is an important aspect to the background of using group methods in training. Working in groups becomes more familiar, so learning in groups becomes more the accepted norm. One must, however, avoid the risk of thinking that group-working is the *only* effective means of teaching, especially considering the staff time involved. Not only do groups move at the speed of the slowest learner, there is also the problem that each group member may have a problem that others do not share, so much time may be spent by the group laboriously reaching only a modest level of learning development.

Leading and other group roles

In all groups the position of the leader is crucial, and in teaching situations the leader is the acknowledged expert in the group, although many leaders may feel no more than competent! The size of the group influences group effectiveness, according to the task. The larger the group, the greater the problems of coordination. Most experienced trainers feel that groups relying mainly on discussion as the means of learning begin to lose their effectiveness if there are more than 12 or 15 members, and that numbers should be lower when the material is particularly difficult. Apprentice classes are able to work with larger numbers, because so much of the learning is practical work by the individual student. Where the group task is not mainly one of social interaction, the size could increase.

The membership of the group will be either reasonably homogeneous, or it will be mixed. Most managers organizing training will be working with homogeneous groups in the sense that they will have a number of points in common, such as membership of the company, or all being recently recruited, or all needing to understand the new computing system. Typically, the leader will probably increase the homogeneity by, for instance, grouping all the supervisors in one group, all the engineers in another and all the marketing staff in a third. Similarity of interests and background aids cooperation and understanding. Mixed group composition is better when the differences of perspective or interest are the core of the training task, because they are differences that have to be overcome, or where a diversity of opinion and expertise is needed to achieve understanding.

Every leader needs to be able to assess the members of the group and work out how to mobilize their diverse competences and contributions to best effect. Here is a recommended approach to running an effective session.

Preparation

Do all members of the group know each other? With a close-knit team, like a senior management group, introductions will obviously not be needed, but there may be a new member of the group, there may be members whose presence puzzles others (or themselves), and sometimes the group will be made up of relative strangers. The group leader has four basic strategies available for making sure that people know each other:

a *Introduce individuals.* Leader makes introductions 'from the chair' of those who are new to those who are established and vice versa, for example: 'I think we know each other, but Ingrid, from Marketing, is with us for the first time. Ingrid, on your right is Roger, from Customer Service, Sheila, from Distribution and Jan, who…'.

b *Ask people to introduce themselves.* 'Could we just go round the group, saying who we are and what our role is…? I'm Simon Legree, from Central Personnel. I've been seconded for three months to act as Trainer on all these sessions. On my right is…?'

c *Ask people to introduce others.* This is a more time-consuming method but can be useful where people have not met before. The leader asks pairs in the group to interview each other for five minutes and then introduce their partner to everyone else. This is particularly useful for a group of strangers, as it initiates discussion and eliminates the self-consciousness felt by many in saying 'I am…'.

d *Wacky methods.* If these approaches are too boring for you, try something novel. Recently I was in a group where the leader began by taking off his shoe, described it briefly and then asked everyone else to do the same. We were all taken aback and started worrying about the condition of our hosiery, but it worked *in that particular situation,* where we all knew each other but the leader was a stranger, who came as a facilitator. He never found out who was who, but got everyone talking. Wacky is risky; take care.

Running the group interaction

The leader sets the scene by reminding everyone of why they have assembled and summarizing what it is they have to do. At this stage members of the group will welcome clear guidance and a suggested structure for the meeting, but the leader will need their consent by signing off with a comment like: 'Is that all right?' 'Is there anything I've missed, do you think?'

The leader now opens the discussion by introducing the topic, or the first of several topics, for the group to develop. There are various ways of doing this:

a *Setting out background information*: adding to the initial introductory comments by providing more general information in a way that will focus the thinking of group members.

b *Providing factual data*: giving group members specific details about the initial topic and inviting their analysis.

c *Offering an opinion*: leading the group towards a conclusion by declaring your own beliefs first is a strong but risky opening. If you are articulating a view that most people will support, the group will make quick progress, but you may prevent people developing true understanding. In your inescapable role as expert, you may not be challenged. If there is likely to be dissent, proceedings will be slowed down, as members of the group first have to grapple with the task of disagreeing with the leader, and then they have to sound out support for their own views.

d *Asking a question*: directing everyone's thinking by posing a question that opens up the topic. It is wise to move from the general to the particular, by setting up the initial discussion around the broader aspects of the question which can later be brought into much sharper focus.

Keeping it moving in the right direction

Although the leader will be less dominant as the discussion gets under way, there is still a need for control and direction, using the following methods:

a *Bringing people in.* Without direction some group members will never speak and others will scarcely stop, but productive discussion will result from a blend of contributions from those in the group whose skill lies in shaping and adding clarity to what others have been saying, or from people who are good at defusing difficult situations. The leader will not only bring in people in a general way ('What do you think, Frank?') but will also shape the discussion by bringing people in for specific comment ('How does John's idea fit in with what you were saying earlier, Helen?'). It is probably not a good idea to include a mild rebuke, such as 'You've been very quiet so far, Liz. Have you no views to share?'

b *Closing people down.* Curbing the voluble is difficult and can make everyone feel awkward if it is not well done, yet the discussion will not work if it is dominated by one or two people. Equally, the trainer will fail if the voluble person is expressing a point of view for which there is broad support, so that the understanding is not moving on. Techniques for the trainer to use in shutting people up are: put one or two closed questions to a person in the middle of a diatribe, give them a job to do ('Could you just jot down for us the main points of that, so that we can come back to it later?'), orient them towards listening ('Are there any problems with what Sheila suggested?').

Closing

There is little need to sustain discussion on matters where everyone is agreed. Agreeing with each other is useful for social cohesion, but the leader needs regularly to direct discussion back to points of disagreement and misunderstanding. It helps to bring in someone who has previously been neutral or silent on the matter and who may therefore have a different perspective.

Periodically the discussion will need to be summarized and a new direction introduced. Members of the group need to confirm the summary. This is usually a job for the leader, but it may be an idea to turn to someone who has been either neutral or silent but attentive ('How would you summarize where we have reached, Wayne?').

Occasionally someone in the group will make a contribution that others do not understand, so the leader will seek clarification, ensuring that the responsibility for the confusion is *not* on the person making the statement. 'Could you just go over that again, Fred?' is better than 'I think what Fred is trying to say is…'.

The session must close and not simply run out of time. It is superficially pleasing when everyone is still keenly discussing when time is up, but it does leave things up in the air. The leader needs to pick out from the discussion one or two workable hypotheses or points of general consensus and put them to the meeting for acceptance. Group members will look to the leader for that type of closure so that they have confirmation that their time has been well spent: only the leader can really see the wood for the trees. The best discussions finish on time!

Coaching and continuous learning

Continuous updating and enrichment of experience is constantly needed for everyone. People who just learn the basics so that they can cope today or this year soon realize that they are finding things too difficult. New ideas are dismissed as ill-founded, new methods are all right for the youngsters but not necessary for those with plenty of experience. As these people fall further and further behind, they become more defiant and more defensive, ignoring the fact that there is a world of difference between 10 years' experience and one year's experience repeated 10 times. Everyone, but especially managers, need continuous learning, to avoid the risk of being left behind. This process is often stimulated and guided by a coach, a colleague who is probably more experienced in the workings of the organization and may be older.

KEY CONCEPT 30

Coaching is a skill in managing a relationship with someone seeking to improve their working performance.

If coaching is to work it needs a mutually respectful relationship between coach and protégé. To some extent a manager is a coach for all those for whom he or she is responsible, but there is always scope for an alternative source of guidance.

A coach needs to understand how learning evolves. An excellent analysis has been produced by Robert Quinn in his work on management skills (Quinn *et al*, 1990). He believes that mastery of an activity involves a learning process that takes place over an extended period of time and that the capacity to learn evolves at the same time. The inference of this is that our approach to organizing facilities for others to learn will be influenced by how far their learning capacity has developed. There are five stages:

1 *The Novice* learns facts and rules without criticism or discussion, accepting that there are ways of doing things that others have devised, and that's that.

2 *The Advanced Beginner* goes a little further by being able to build in lessons from experience, so that understanding begins to expand and to fill out

basic facts and rules. As you begin working in an organization, you begin to see how cultural norms are just as important as the basic rules. You find out the subtleties of working relationships and extend competence by trying out very slight departures from the rigidity of the rules.

3 *Competency* represents a further development of confidence and a reduced reliance on absolute rules by recognizing a wider variety of cues from the working context. There is a greater degree of learning by trial and error, experimenting with new behaviours. It is not abandoning the rules, but being able to use them more imaginatively and with an interpretation that suits one's own personal strengths and inclinations.

4 *Proficiency* is where the learner transcends analysis to being able to use intuition: 'Calculation and rational analysis seem to disappear. The unconscious, fluid, and effortless performance begins to emerge, and no one plan is held sacred. You learn to unconsciously "read" the evolving situation. You notice cues and respond to new cues as the importance of the old ones recede' (Quinn *et al*, 1990: 315).

5 *Expert* is the term used to describe those rare people who produce masterly performance simply by doing what comes naturally, because all the learning has fused together to develop a capacity based on having in their heads 'multidimensional maps of the territory' that are unknown to other people and they are thus able to meet effortlessly the contradictions of organizational life.

You may dismiss that as an academic playing with words in order to say nothing very much, but I think it is a neat and helpful model that can be an encouragement to anyone to take on the idea of continuous learning as a way of valuing the opportunities that their work offers for their own personal development and enrichment. There is still a risk that some people become complacent in their assessment of their own expertise and fail to see that there has been a sea change that undermines the expert's certainties. There is always a temptation for established managers to take short cuts on the basis of their assumed expertise without realizing that the rules have been changed, so that they are playing the wrong game. Good coaches puncture complacency without deflating self-esteem.

Reference

Quinn, RE, Faerman, SR, Thompson, MP and McGrath, MR (1990) *Becoming a Master Manager*, John Wiley & Sons, Inc, Hoboken, NJ.

FURTHER READING

Quinn, RE (1988) *Beyond Rational Management: Mastering the paradoxes and competing demands of high performance*, Jossey-Bass, San Francisco.

Chapter Ten
Performance

Getting the right results from the people you work with

William Shakespeare put his opinion about King Henry VIII into a speech by the first of his six wives, Catherine of Aragon: 'His promises were, as he then was, mighty; but his performance, as he is now, nothing.'

The same sentiment is frequently expressed by managers, although less elegantly, about members of staff for whom they are responsible. So often it seems that promise is not fulfilled in performance. Also, people often seem to lack the confidence or the application to fulfil their potential. Central to the effectiveness of every manager is the need to conjure an effective performance from their people. Perhaps the most difficult situation is where the manager has a staff member who has run out of steam or who feels misused by circumstances. For a long time there has been intemperate discussion by journalists and politicians about the need 'to root out bad teachers' but never a word about recovering teachers who have lost their way.

At the beginning of this trend, colleagues of mine and I were commissioned to undertake research on the problem of underperformance by teachers. The broad conclusions were disappointing, but not surprising. The standard comment among school heads about underperforming teachers was some euphemism for 'get rid of them'. Rarely was the problem of an underperforming teacher seen as a problem of underperformance to be solved; it was a problem of the teacher who should be got rid of. A puzzle about values in school teaching is that great efforts are made to deal with underperformance among children, but little among staff except for long periods of sickness absence. One shining example was a head who had worked hard at recovering the confidence and effectiveness of a 54-year-old teacher and showed me a letter from her which included the following: 'Thank you for all you have done for me this year... You have given me my life back'.

This chapter is shorter than earlier ones because many features have already been covered in earlier chapters, such as 4, 7 and 9, or in those still to come, such as 13, 18 and 19. How do you pull off this trick of enabling people to perform?

Getting the right people in the right jobs. If you are picking them, make absolutely sure that they are the right ones, or that their small deviations from your ideal are things you can deal with or work round. If you didn't pick them, work hard at getting them on side. Remembering Chapter 4, work hard at getting each one in the right job, role or whatever is the appropriate descriptor, exploit their skills, experience and aspirations. As far as possible, give them the scope and resources they need. Explain what you can't do, but only after you have tried one more time. If they ask for something you feel is not necessary, tell them why.

The right lines of communication. What they need to know, the key people for their personal network and some ideas on how best to work it.

These introductory points lead on to managing the ongoing performance of the person once everything is in place to enable them to perform. Perhaps your business has a system of performance management in place to help you with this. Performance management is the current vogue and it has many merits, emphasizing future rather than past performance and recognizing the importance of planning, with goals and standards, appropriate resources, guidance and support from the individual's manager all being essential to the fundamental objective of focusing people's individual ability and motivation to produce a performance in line with the needs of the business. That gives us five points to look at in a little more detail.

Planning, goals and standards. Effective performance is *planned* to provide a framework for your working future; it helps make the future happen while payments for achieving specific targets reward past performance.

I deliberately use the term 'goal' rather than 'target' because the current use of targets is trying to find markers of achievement that are measurable and for which a person is accountable. This is to ensure focus on meeting a target that is so precise that there can be no argument about success or failure and attaching to it a financial payment. This was because of a tendency, in practice, for the money to be paid even if the target had not been hit, or if there were all manner of extenuating circumstances of the 'it wasn't my fault' type. I am not advocating cleverer or more complicated methods of payment, but concentrating narrowly on performance. Never forget that performance is one of the most effective motivators; relating payment to specific performance measures is a distraction both from overall performance and from job satisfaction. People at work are relatively satisfied or dissatisfied with what they are paid. They are relatively satisfied or dissatisfied with their jobs by a number of different factors: the intrinsic quality of the work they have to do, the quality of working relationships, especially their boss, the quality of the organizational culture, pride in their company and its products, and many other factors. Everyone at work needs some degree of being told what to do. In the introductory chapter you met Fred the service engineer. He was the right person in the right job with the lines of communication that he needed. He was told what to do on a daily basis with his schedule of visits. Tomorrow does not yet exist. In contrast, Helen works within some frameworks that tell her what to do in the whole school year, like the syllabus and the level of pupil achievement that has to be reached, according to standards that are both externally determined, like the number of GCSEs that each child should reach, and improvement targets that may have been specified by central government or the schools' inspectorate or the school timetable. Then there are the short-term or immediate plans for individual lesson periods or attainment targets for individual children. Plans and targets for the short and longer term are normally agreed between managers and those who report to them, with a gap between agreeing them and reviewing them, the length of the gap varying between relatively long for jobs that justify considerable discretion and relatively short for jobs that require frequent monitoring by someone else.

Appropriate resources. People need appropriate resources to perform effectively. Some are organized by the individual, like getting a new printer cartridge, and others have to be arranged by their manager because the decisions needed to provide the resource are 'above my pay grade'. The manager is central in deciding whether it is needed or could be done some other way and then arguing the case with other people or arguing a different case with the individual who is not going to get the resource. This helps the planning to be a joint activity with one's boss.

Guidance and support from one's manager. 'What, more? They've got the job and the right resources. We've agreed the targets. Surely they just have to get on and deliver?' This is only partly true. Some roles in the business require minimal support from a boss, especially jobs of the lone professional type, like a medical officer in a factory or a legal adviser, but they still need some, and everyone working with other people has basic human needs for reassurance that they are doing well and their performance is valued. Occasionally they will value having the benefit of talking over ways of dealing with a problem. Letting off steam with a spouse may be effective, but talking things through with one's manager is probably of more practical value as you both have an interest in you performing well.

Support is valued when it comes from other colleagues, not just from one's manager. Colleagues who do the same job, or one that is very similar, are an admirable source of encouragement because they know the challenges. Ron Grainger is a teacher of physics who had spent most of his working life in the engineering industry before making a career change in his fifties to teach in a secondary school, so in one way he was a novice but he was also a person who had succeeded in a different career and had a calm cheerfulness throughout his working day, thoroughly enjoying his teaching. He readily acknowledged his lack of experience and genuinely admired the achievements of his colleagues, regularly asking how they approached particular aspects of the curriculum or particular pupils. The Head of Science said: 'Ron is great. I can be a bit blunt at times with the science teachers and make what they regard as unreasonable demands and get their backs up. After a particularly awkward staff meeting last week I heard Ron say, "It'll all look different on Monday", which calmed everyone down.'

KEY CONCEPT 31

For effective performance to come from your people they need (a) to be the right people in the right job, (b) the right lines of communication, (c) planning, goals and standards, (d) guidance and support from you and (e) appraisal.

Appraisal is not enough on its own, but is a central feature in generating, maintaining and refreshing performance. It is different from the regular conversations that managers hold with their people because there is a degree of formality in the process with which managers and their people have to comply. The main advantage of this external creation of the system is that it prevents too much cosiness, which can make the exchanges too comfortable, avoiding some of the harder issues that need to be faced. It is a review and discussion about the past in order to plan what is to come, dealing with problems that still have not gone away and producing more creative solutions. In Part 2 there is a chapter on conducting the appraisal. The reason for slotting this bit here is to argue that the appraisal process is essential to managing performance.

Managing the boss. The idea of managing one's boss may sound like a contradiction. 'Surely it's my boss's job to manage me?' No; it is very limited to regard the relationship with the organizational superior as one in which they tell you what to do and you respond with deference or what the Americans call 'apple polishing'. It is even more limited to regard the relationship as one in which the subordinate aims to comply precisely with what the manager asks for and then awaits further instructions, so that the job is satisfactorily done when the wishes of the boss have been met. Virtually all the jobs that people hold are those in which there are a range of responsibilities, accountabilities and obligations, both formal and informal. Also, all jobs require some skill and some initiative, and the more autonomous a job is, the less precise is the nature and degree of the supervision provided by the manager.

The relationship with the boss is not only crucial to effectiveness and personal well-being, it also has to be managed by both parties. This is not political manoeuvring or apple polishing, but consciously working with the boss to obtain better results. The relationship is not master and servant, but a relationship of two servants, relating to each other via a third point in a triangular affiliation, which is the task on which they are both engaged: the customers they seek to serve or the stakeholders they seek to satisfy.

The process is mainly one of mutual accommodation and adjustment, as the two parties find the best way to share duties between them. They start from the position that the boss has, for instance, more formal power and access to more extensive information, while the subordinate may have better grapevine information and a more flexible programme of work. To this will then be added the advantages that each has in terms of personal qualities, qualifications and experience. By discussion and getting used to each other, both boss and subordinate can improve their joint and individual results, but it needs initiative from both of them; not just from the boss.

The subordinate realizes that the boss can influence the promotion and career development prospects of the subordinate, and this will always limit the degree of candour in everyday exchanges. It also illuminates the need for the subordinate to work within the consent, or the tacit consent, of the boss when taking initiatives. In this way there will be support in times of difficulty and a greater likelihood that decisions on action are well judged. Sometimes the boss has to be used to get things changed. It may be anything from an administrative procedure that is not working or policies about particular clients that need changing to tasks traditionally associated with one's job that no longer seem appropriate. Subordinates often assume that bosses know what the subordinate's job involves and what is happening within its framework, when actually they do not know at all. A useful tactic is to keep the boss advised of what is irritating or frustrating. In doing this, however, it is well to remember the transactional analysis idea of Carl Rogers. The subordinate is more likely to be successful if the conversations with the boss are adult-to-adult transactions, rather than those of the bad-tempered child whining to the uninterested parent. There is also the range of tactics that are involved in organizational politics: reciprocal support for a patron.

KEY CONCEPT 32

Managing the boss is an integral part of producing effective performance; people management is not all one way.

FURTHER READING

For a general discussion of method and practice in managing
    performance the main authority is Armstrong, M and Baron, A
    (2005) *Managing Performance: Performance management
    in action,* CIPD, London. Two general reviews of practice
    are CIPD (2005) *Performance Management: Survey Report,*
    CIPD, London, and IDS (2005) *IDS Studies: Performance
    Management,* No. 796, April, IDS, London.
Towards the end of the chapter there is a reference to adult-to-
    adult conversations being more productive than those that
    are like parent-to-child. This refers to work by the American
    psychotherapist, Carl Rogers, in his work on counselling. After
    Freud he is the most influential psychotherapist of the 20th
    century. He is most accessible through Thorne, B (1992)
    Carl Rogers (Key Figures in Counselling and Psychotherapy
    series), Sage, London.

Part Two
How to...

Chapter Eleven
How to analyse your management job

One method of organizing one's time is to analyse how it is spent by using a temporary diary method to note down what is being done and how long it takes. You can then review the proportion of time spent over several days on various activities and decide whether or not this is how the time should be spent. To do this you need to group different activities into categories. The suggested method is that described in Chapter 1 as sSAMp.

KEY CONCEPT 6 (AGAIN)

The central elements of the work that managers do can be classified as specialist, administrative or managerial. The balance between these three varies between different jobs and even between people with jobs that are notionally identical. Each manager needs to consider very carefully the balance between the three that will lead to effective performance and job satisfaction.

Here is a reminder:

s. Lower-case s stands for social, the bundle of mainly social things that people do during the working day.

S. The first capital letter stands for specialist. This is the work managers do because of their basic profession, working experience or qualification. It is also the work

done by their subordinate, a capital S because this is a
central part of the manager's responsibilities and crucial
to the working relationship with colleagues.

A. This is for administrative and covers all the
straightforward duties of organization maintenance.

M. Managerial work is creating precedents or taking other
steps to innovate: making things happen that would not
otherwise happen.

p. Finally, a lower-case p for personal. Everyone has to go
to the loo, but there are other matters to deal with, and
local custom and practice will vary.

Every manager's day will be taken up with activities that fall
into each of these categories and the analysis comes from
comparing, especially those that are S, A or M, although you
may be interested in how much time you spend on the other
two. You need a simple form to note for each activity: the time
it began, what it was, in brief personal shorthand, whether it
was initiated by self or other and whether it was S, A, or M. The
first thing to notice is the proportion of your time that is spent
responding to others and the proportion spent in you taking
initiatives, sometimes known as reactive and proactive. There
is no standard for this, as jobs vary so enormously. The nurse
in charge of an A&E department of a hospital has to wait for
accidents and emergencies to happen; there is no question of
going out to make them happen, but there is still much potential
for M-type initiatives in internal organization and methods. The
key is whether they are necessary and will improve the service
the department provides. Sales managers can rarely just wait for
the orders to roll in. Not only do they constantly need to identify
fresh customers and introduce new products, they need to
monitor the sales mix to ensure there is an appropriate balance
between low-margin and high-margin lines. For every individual
there is the question, what do you think of that balance? Are
you responding too often and initiating too rarely, or have you
got it right?

The next step is to examine the S–A–M distribution of time. The range found in research was wide, but did not neatly match the type of job. Senior managers do not necessarily have the highest M. Jobs such as supervisor of motorway repair teams and design and development engineers in cutting-edge electronics typically had among the highest proportion of M – more than those in management jobs one or two grades above them. Those at the top of small hierarchies had relatively high M. Head teachers, for instance, generally had a higher proportion of M (ranging from 27 to 82 per cent, with an average of 60.7 per cent) than their deputies (range: 4 to 76 per cent, average: 39.3 per cent). Whatever the job, the distribution was significantly affected by the predilections of the individual managers and it is certainly something they can influence.

Individual managers are nearly always surprised by how much time they spend on administration, as defined. Recommendations are:

a Squeeze A into the smallest amount of time possible without making mistakes. Do not make it into a full job and never create A work for others unless it is really necessary.

b Never lose touch with S, as this is the strongest source of respect from your subordinates. It is what they do all day. The manager who keeps in touch with it, can talk the talk and appreciate what is going on, will be on the way to having a team who respect their manager.

c Build up M, as this is what builds a career and makes a managerial job worthwhile.

It is difficult to measure what makes for job satisfaction and career progress, but I am convinced that these simple guidelines are key to success in both satisfaction and progress for managerial jobs of all types and at all levels.

Chapter Twelve
How to develop your network

Key Concept 4 introduced the core tasks of managers as being to develop a series of agendas, or things to do, and networks, contacts outside the business as well as inside, to help you implement your agenda. The formal hierarchy within the business is typically described by an organization chart that specifies where people fit in the pattern of working relationships and where key decision making is located. For any manager this is the starting point as you figure out where you fit in and where you go to for approvals or sign-offs, for advice or for information. The limitations of organization charts are their encouragement of formality, and the fact that they are always out of date. The telephone directory may be more reliable.

Individual managers develop their own networks of informal contacts which they use to improve their ability to decide what to do, to get things done and to extend their knowledge of the working world they inhabit. This is different from, but compatible with, the formal structure, mainly because it extends beyond the organizational boundary of the business.

Networks are cooperative relationships of people who can help each other accomplish things and the contact method is most likely to be face to face or telephone rather than memo or electronic. This is, of course, a norm of everyday life at home. When a radiator starts to leak, you ask Ronnie if he knows a plumber; worrying about where your 4-year-old should go for swimming lessons, you ask Frieda or Jonty. An early priority of moving to a new home is to begin a network of exactly these sorts of contact. For managers the network is likely to be larger and more diverse, with dozens or hundreds of people on it. It is for sharing ideas, information and advice. It is much better than the formal hierarchy in that it provides horizontal links and is status-blind. It is not the same as an old-boy network, which is to capitalize on the benefits shared exclusively by a specific group of people. The manager's network is larger, always looking for new members and essential for getting things done.

Developing a network

A network is developed by using the facilities which the managerial life provides:

Conferences and courses. From the list of attendees you spot people who look interesting, identify them round the table, listen to what they say and bump into them at coffee break or in the bar after dinner.

Travel. One aspect of working life for many managers is sitting next to strangers for many hours while travelling. Initially the only communication is grunts, but take a peek at what they are reading; if it strikes a chord it could be a conversation opener. If you are on a flight that includes a meal (yes, some airlines still do this), then conversation with someone so physically close is almost essential to cover the furtive shuffles both of you are making to avoid the other's thigh. Warnings: (a) unsolicited approaches from someone of the opposite sex can be misconstrued, (b) if the other person is making heavy weather of the crossword, resist the temptation of pointing out that one across is 'transcendentalism'.

The photocopier/printer. Offices typically have a printer and/or photocopier shared by a number of people, who welcome the chance to escape from where they should be for a few minutes and exchange pleasantries with other people about what is wrong with the world. You discover that Emma is in Marketing and Charles runs Logistics.

Books, papers, minutes and newsletters. Reading stuff related to your world of work may provide useful information for you on widget making or whatever, but it also includes names of potential recruits to your network.

The grapevine. Workplaces thrive on rumour and speculation, especially on matters that those involved wish to keep confidential: '... strictly between you and me ...' is a guarantee that what you are about to say is shared with several others within the hour. If you feel you are above mere gossip-mongering, remember that gossip is mainly about people, so you hear that Fred Bloggs is close to a deal with XYZ Ltd and that ABC Ltd have failed to entice Sally Blenkinsop away to run their Leeds office.

Mentors and protégés. As people in a business acquire more experience and seniority, they may take an informal interest in the careers of others with whom they have worked satisfactorily before and so become their unofficial mentor, willing to offer advice or endorse in subtle ways a protégé. Because of working together previously, protégés have confidence in the mentor and will incidentally provide information about developments elsewhere that the mentor finds useful.

Professional bodies and networks. If you are a member of a professional body that has meetings in your locality, attending such meetings can produce the same sort of contacts as attending courses and conferences. Some social networking sites specialize in professional people.

Building the network

These are just a few of the ways in which you identify possible members of your network, but what next? You have to remember that a network is a relationship between people seeking an advantage and, to use an over-used cliché, '… there's no such thing as a free lunch'. You have to be both able and willing to respond to requests as well as make them, although not necessarily at the same time; you can build up credit.

Building relationships with network members is a straightforward social skill, but some are much more socially skilful than others. If you are brash, assertive and try to dominate others, you may not get much from your network, although you will probably succeed in other ways. If you are an introvert who hates meeting new people, networking is probably not for you, although you will acquire a small number of very good contacts. Assuming you are not brash or introvert, rarely try to dominate others and quite like meeting new people, you will probably find it easy to build your network, but some suggestions may help:

- Focus first on people you feel dependent on and get to know them better, perhaps by doing a small favour.

- Establish your reputation as a good team player, a good listener, a reliable source of information, or all three. Don't tell people, don't show off, just display the behaviours that will lead others to build your reputation for you.

- Practise 'working a room'. Where people are standing around, individually or in groups during the tea break on a course or similar situation, move round progressively between groups of two. Spot two people who are talking to each other but without showing signs of mutual engagement. If they are almost side by side, looking outwards, go up to them directly with a friendly smile and start a conversation on something vaguely relevant ('I found that quite useful, but do you think there will be more question and answer later?'). Move on to direct questions about them ('You're the person from Shell, aren't you?' or 'Have you got a particular interest today?'). When you have got what you want, notice someone else in the room and move on.

- Business cards: the office-issue business card that is the same as everyone else's doesn't cost you anything and is obviously official, emphasizing the business brand. If you have any control over the way your personal particulars are presented, concentrate on what helps people put you in their network. Normally omit qualifications unless they are an essential element of your role and indicate specific, key features that are widely acknowledged, like Chartered Accountant or Chartered Engineer. Take care also with titles that vaguely indicate status, but not in a way that is helpful. Senior Section Manager may mean a lot to you but little to the person you meet on a course. Always have your cards with you, in mint condition.

- Organize and use your network. Organizing seems to vary infinitely between individuals. The smartphone or electronic personal organizer is popular, but other people keep a stack of business cards held together with an elastic band. Others rely on memory. Whatever your method is, make it easy to refer to frequently and use it.

KEY CONCEPT 33

Methods of building your network include getting to know better those on whom you feel dependent, developing a reputation as a good team player (by deeds not words), practising working a room and using business cards.

Chapter Thirteen
How to organize your department

This short chapter picks up on the points made at the close of Chapter 4, suggesting a sequence of questions on departmental organization about purpose, activities, grouping, authority, and connections. We now need to think a bit further on practical implementation within your individual department. You will rarely have the luxury of creating an organization for a department from scratch. Much more common is reorganizing around one or more people who have left, probably not being immediately replaced, or coping with a demand from somewhere else to reduce the departmental headcount by x per cent. The starting point is still to think about the requisite structure, *not the people*. You may modify your ideas when you move on to thinking about the people, but the basic, inescapable reality is that organizing round the people never works, even in the most freewheeling of the creative industries. Modifying (not changing) the structure to accommodate and exploit individual competences can succeed as long as it does not distort.

Now start thinking through the desired structure within the constraints you are stuck with, using the following checklist as a start.

Checklist for thinking about the organization of a department

The PURPOSE of the department

a Does it either meet a basic business need or help to make things run more smoothly? Is it necessary?

b Is it set up on the basis of output, like business objectives to be achieved, or on the basis of inputs, like people and problems? Are the outputs already being produced elsewhere?

c Does the department exist to deal with matters which other managers find uninteresting or unattractive? If 'yes', are the reasons good enough?

The ACTIVITIES to meet the purpose

a Does the section bring together those who share a particular skill or those with a particular responsibility?

b What activities have to be carried out to meet the purpose?

c How many people with what experience and qualifications are needed for those activities?

d How many ancillary employees are needed? How can that number be reduced? How can that number be reduced further?

e Are all the identified activities needed? Is there any duplication with other sections and departments? Is there a better way?

GROUPING the activities

a How much specialization is needed? How will this specialization affect job satisfaction, commitment and efficiency?

b Are boundaries between jobs clearly defined and in the right place? Are they necessary?

c Will job holders have the amount of discretion needed to be effective?

The AUTHORITY of job holders

a Do job titles and other 'labels' indicate satisfactorily the authority of the job holder?

b Do all job holders have the necessary equipment, like keys, passwords and information for their duties?

c Do all job holders have the required authorizations, like authorization to sign documents, that are needed?

d Is the authority of any job holder unreasonably restricted?

CONNECTING the activities of job holders

a Do job holders know what they need to know about the activities of their colleagues?

b Are there enough meetings of staff, too few or too many?

Once you have worked through this list you should have a picture of what you need to achieve. Ask yourself one more question: is that really what you think is the best arrangement?

TABLE 13.1 Cost/benefit analysis

Costs	Benefits
Redundancies/compensation/ effect on morale of remaining staff	Deadwood removed
Training	Necessary new skills/attitudes developed
Salary adjustments	Consolidation of new skills/ attitudes
New equipment	Increased potential of remaining staff
Replacement staff	Necessary new skills/attitudes acquired

If not, fiddle a bit more until it is. Now do a quick, rough-and-ready cost/benefit analysis, not only in financial terms, for example as shown in Table 13.1.

That is just to illustrate the approach. Every situation is different and you will need to work out the criteria that meet your situation; what is essential is that you set up material to justify the changes to the people who will need to be convinced.

Consulting the boss. Now start selling your *tentative* proposal. Start with your boss, emphasizing that it is not in concrete, but to get the reaction. The boss's perspective will be different from yours and you will probably come away from the meeting having been told that some things will not fly at all. As long as you have always managed your boss properly (remember the end of Chapter 10), you will also come away with some constructive suggestions and offers of help.

Consulting the staff. The first step with the affected staff depends on whether or not there are redundancies to be made. If there are, deal with them first so that subsequently you are dealing with those who are staying, not leaving. Dealing with making people redundant is neither easy nor pleasant. The method and approach will be determined by the HR people, and you will have to follow their suggestions closely. You may think their approach is stupid; you may think the HR people are stupid, but they are carrying the can and this is a matter on which you really cannot afford to be isolated.

Once that unpleasantness is out of the way, at least for you and your continuing colleagues, you need to consult with your staff face to face and preferably one to one, although there may be a preliminary meeting of everybody to air insecurities, grievances and resentment. Your necessary message is one of reassurance ('Maybe we were hard on Phil and Angela, and we will have some problems in adjusting to the new situation, but you are all staying and you're staying because we need you'). Everyone will then want to know what happens next, but you cannot answer the question. So far you have some ideas and some general guidance from the boss, but you are going to talk to everyone to make sure that you get the best possible outcome. Remember Key Concept 2.

Talking to individuals will go one of two ways. Some will see opportunities ('... especially now Phil has gone...'). Others will see threats to their sense of security because of the need to learn new skills, not knowing how they will cope without Angela, or even whether they will have to work harder. Most of them will also hope for a pay rise.

Sketch out your tentative ideas for them, asking how they could be improved. Dismiss none of their suggestions at this stage, pointing out the difficulties – but not impossibilities – of some and talking others through further. Make no commitments at this stage, but reshape your original plan to use suggestions that can be incorporated to improve it.

Have one more quick chat with the boss and proceed to what is needed for your proposals to be accepted so that you can get on with making it all happen.

Chapter Fourteen
How to cope with committees

An engineering plant manager has on the wall of his office a framed citation confirming that he is a full member of 'The Institution of Meetings Engineers'. This non-existent body was dreamt up by a few engineers who felt that most meetings were a waste of time. The inscription included phrases such as: 'Members shall attend all meetings called, regardless of their value... Any member falling asleep shall have membership suspended until he wakes up... A member finding a meeting useful should send a full report to the General Secretary of the Institution before seeking medical attention.'

Meetings are an inescapable part of the management process and they are frequently less successful than they should be, leading to the cynicism of The Institution of Meetings Engineers. They take a lot of time, so how do you at least cope and perhaps make good use of the meetings you attend? The basic necessities are a clear format, purpose and preparation, with the leader being in control. Those attending the meeting can then concentrate on content rather than fretting about the way the meeting is being conducted. People will only attend and make a success of meetings they see as useful. Poor meetings not only fail to achieve objectives, they also do harm, as members become frustrated about lack of progress or about not being able to get their point of view across. It is not just the fault of the person in charge: all participants have to learn meeting mechanics. The analogy of the orchestra is apt. The conductor is responsible for the quality of the coordinated act, but every instrumentalist has to make a distinctive, but not individualistic, contribution that blends with all the others.

Chairing

Chairing is a position that is associated with authority. Company boards, benches of magistrates, cabinet committees, employment tribunals, political parties, debating societies are among the many activities that are led by the person in the chair. Professors in universities are appointed to chairs, not because they are too weary or lazy to stand up, but because the occupation of a chair represents authority. If you are chairing a meeting, be sure you know the answer to some preliminary questions:

1 Does this meeting have the power to take a decision, to make a recommendation, or simply to exchange information? All of these are equally valid objectives, but it helps to be clear on this basic question of what sort of meeting it is.

2 What should the agenda be? The content of the agenda is usually drafted and proposed by the chair or, in more formal meetings, the chair in consultation with the secretary. The topics need to be clearly described, so that members of the group can come to the meeting with an understanding of them and with a focus on the key issues. The sequence of items is a question of which chicken needs to come before which egg. Getting the right things early on the agenda can make it easier to resolve later matters provided they are in the right order; otherwise decisions are half made and then deferred 'until we have dealt with item X'.

3 What is the meeting for? It may be to convey information. Then the sole focus is on the chair, who is passing on information or analysis or news to a gathering of those who need to know. The only role for others attending the meeting is to listen, perhaps ask questions and probably mutter explanations and reiterations to each other to check their understanding. The reason for doing this in a meeting rather than by e-mail or memorandum is to give the opportunity for further clarification through questions; there is also the symbolic impact of information being passed on personally rather than impersonally. It is therefore usually done for matters of weight and significance.

4 If a meeting is to share information, the chair is the coordinator rather than the fount of all wisdom. A health or social work case conference is a typical example and the chair needs skill to elicit constructive participation, and to encourage a free flow of information at the same time as preventing such a free flow that the meeting becomes chaotic and loses any sense of direction.

5 At a meeting to make a decision, the expertise needed to make the right decision is distributed among the members of the group, so that much of the time is spent sharing information, but there has to be joint ownership of, or support for, the decision that is eventually made. This is most often by consensus to be identified as the discussion develops so that it can be articulated for everyone to accept or modify until it wins general acceptance and commitment. Some decisions are reached by voting. Although these are not common in management meetings, it is still essential that the chair moves to a vote only when a consensus is apparent. A majority of one is scarcely a majority at all and talking should continue until the weight of opinion is more substantial.

KEY CONCEPT 34

A person chairing a meeting needs to answer these questions: (1) Is the purpose of this meeting to decide, to recommend or to share information? (2) What should the agenda be? (3) What can I expect to be achieved at this meeting? (4) How can I chair the meeting in a way that is most effective for the agenda and to achieve my objective?

Conduct of the meeting itself

Few people are accustomed to expressing a point of view in a meeting, and many find it inhibiting. They speak best when asked to do so, and when speaking on something about which they are knowledgeable. Leaders of meetings get contributions by asking people to speak, picking up non-verbal cues of a desire to speak or reaction to what someone else has said. Statements of fact rather than expressions of opinion are the easiest way for people to make their first contribution. Experienced members of groups can help the less experienced by 'shaping' the clumsy or over-emotional comments of their colleagues and agreeing with them (for example: 'I would like to agree with what Hilary was saying and make the further point ...', *not* 'I think Hilary was trying to say...').

Curbing the excesses of the verbose is a true test of chairing skill. Making a succinct and focused contribution is a competence not found often among people attending meetings, so the chair has to be skilled not only in eliciting contributions, but also in closing people down when they are running out of control. Here are some suggestions: (1) Use eye contact with the speaker to indicate encouragement or discouragement. When you begin to lose interest, or become mildly irritated, the speaker will receive that silent message and will usually respond to it. (2) For those who will not respond, use more direct signals, such as looking away or looking anxiously at your watch. (3) Use focus questions. If the speaker is rambling on and on, direct what is being said by interrupting with a question to focus the speaker and to elicit an answer that is likely to be brief.

Bringing people into the discussion at the time when their contribution is most appropriate can be done by picking out someone who you think should have a relevant or constructive comment to make and put a direct question to them ('What is your view, Henry?' or 'I wonder if Sheila could help us with the exact figures ...' or 'Well, I know that Harry has direct experience of this sort of problem...').

As the meeting proceeds, the chair is constantly listening and looking for relevant contributions as a pattern develops which the chair then helps everyone to see and concentrate on.

The rank and file member of the committee

Chairing is the key role in a committee, but what about the rest? First of all, the other people are not quite equal. Some are more rank than file. Some are much involved in dealing with whatever the committee decides, while others may not have any direct interest and may well wonder why they are there at all. So you first need to work out your role, as that will affect how you behave. Are you, for instance, sage, brake, technical adviser, synthesizer, stimulus, delegate, diplomat or something else? Probably you may combine two or three of those roles. Whatever you decide will shape your approach and behaviour.

Some general suggestions are: (1) Be objective in seeking solutions that others will accept. (2) Support and develop contributions from others that you regard as being constructive. (3) Constantly monitor the mood of the meeting to judge when best to make your contributions, facts, opinions, suggestions or hypotheses. (4) Always work through the chair, recognizing the authority that the group always invests in that role, even in informal meetings.

KEY CONCEPT 35

Rank and file members of the meeting can make their best contributions by: (1) looking for solutions that others will support; (2) building on contributions from others that they regard as constructive; (3) monitoring the mood of the meeting to judge when best to make your contributions; (4) working through the chair.

Chapter Fifteen
How to make a presentation

At least nine out of every ten of you who have been good enough to read this book will have experienced one or more awful presentations. Presentation is a simple thing to do, but few people take the time to do it properly. Some of the common blunders are: the speaker is inaudible, incoherent, mumbles, does not look at the audience, goes too fast, always speaks in a monotone and constantly repeats nonsense words to fill gaps, the most common being 'you know', 'as it were', 'to be perfectly honest with you', 'quite frankly', 'as I was saying', 'er'. The visual aids are too small, too crowded, clearly prepared for a different audience, and cluttered up with clever gimmicks which the speaker has discovered on the PC and which he or she uses to distract from the message that the visual aids are trying to convey. All too often they are also the speaker's only notes, so he or she simply reads out loud what the audience have already read from the screen.

Presentation is to inform and explain to a group of people. Managers constantly have to present on such matters as explaining a change of policy, the implications of organizational alteration, pitching to a senior management group for an improvement in the budget, 'selling' the advantages of a new performance management scheme, or explaining to a small group of job applicants the details of the post for which they have applied.

Objectives

As with almost every aspect of management, the starting point is the objective. What are you aiming to achieve? What do you want the listeners to do, to think or to feel? The question is *not* 'What do you want to say?' The objective is in the response of the listeners. That starting point begins the whole process with a focus on results and payoff, turning attention away from ego. It also determines tone. If your objective is to inform, you will emphasize facts. If you aim to persuade, you will try to appeal to emotion as well as to reason.

The material

What is to be said or, more accurately, what should the audience go away having understood and remembered? Organize your material with an introduction that previews, a body that develops, and a conclusion that reviews. Start with the theme. This is a planning device that holds together the various ideas you want to discuss. If the theme of your presentation is informative, the body should provide facts. If the theme is persuasive, the body should develop persuasive arguments.

In the introduction the speaker establishes a relationship with the audience. Apart from gaining their attention, the speaker will include here an answer to the unspoken question: Is it going to be worth our while listening? Is this person worth listening to? The person who is worth listening to is someone who looks at the audience and looks friendly, knowledgeable and, above all, enthusiastic. A useful format for the introduction is to explain what the members of the audience will know or be able to do at the end. It is also helpful to sketch out the framework of what is to come, so that people can follow it more readily. But stick to what you promise. If you say there are going to be five points, the audience will listen for five to make sure that they have not missed one. Having secured the attention of the listeners, they now wait not just for what you say next, but with a framework in their heads of what they will hear, so as to locate their understanding within that framework.

The main body of the presentation is the message that is to be conveyed, the development of the argument and the build-up of what it is that the audience should go away having understood and remembered. It will be organized not only to help the audience maintain attention, but also to discipline the speaker to avoid rambling, distracting irrelevance or forgetting. The most common methods are:

Chronological sequence, perhaps taking the audience through a series of events such as disappointing sales results last year leading to some sales redundancies, some improvement in recent months and new products, new recruits, general need for retraining alongside advertising campaign starting next month...

Known to unknown, or simple to complex. Starting with a brief review of what the audience already know or can easily understand and then developing to what they do not yet know or cannot yet understand. The logic of this method is to ground the audience in something they can handle so that they can make sense of the unfamiliar.

Problem to solution is almost the exact opposite of simple to complex. A problem is presented and a solution follows. The understanding of the audience is again grounded, but this time grounded in an anxiety that the speaker is about to relieve.

Comparison is a method which compares one account with another. Selling often follows this path, as the new is compared with the old.

Whatever way the material is organized, the main body will always contain a number of key thoughts or ideas. This is what the speaker is trying to plant in the minds of the audience: not just facts, which are inert, but the ideas which facts may well illustrate and clarify. The idea that inflation is dangerously high is only illustrated by the fact that it is at a particular figure in a particular month.

The ideas in a presentation can be helpfully linked together by a device that will help audience members to remember them and to grasp their interdependence. One method is to enshrine the ideas in a story. If the story is recalled, the thoughts are recalled with it, as they are integral to the structure. Another method is to use key words to identify the points that are being made, especially if they have an alliterative or mnemonic feature, such as 'People Produce Prosperity'. In a lecture it is common to provide a framework for ideas by using a drawing or system model to show the interconnection of points.

Facts, by giving impact, keep together the framework of ideas that the speaker has assembled. They clarify and give dimension to what is being said. The danger is to use too many, so that the audience are overwhelmed by facts and figures which begin to bemuse them. If the presentation is to be accompanied by a handout, facts may be usefully contained in that, so that they can be referred to later, without the audience having to remember them.

Humour is dangerous. If the audience laugh at a funny story, the speaker will be encouraged and may feel under less tension, but how tempting to try again and end up 'playing for laughs'. Laughter is a most seductive human reaction, but too many laughs are even more dangerous than too many facts. What will the audience remember: the joke, or what the joke was intended to illustrate? Attempted humour is also dangerous for the ineffective comedian. If you tell what you think is a funny story and no one laughs, you have made a fool of yourself (at least in your own eyes) and risk floundering.

Very few people speak effectively without notes. Although there is a tendency to marvel at those who can, relying solely on memory risks missing something out, getting a fact wrong or drying up completely. Notes follow the pattern of organization you have established, providing discipline and limiting the tendency to ramble. It is both irritating and unhelpful for an audience to cope with a speaker who wanders off down a blind alley. When an amusing anecdote pops up in your brain, it can be almost irresistible to share it.

There are two basic kinds of notes: headlines or a script. Headlines are probably the most common, with main points underlined and facts listed beneath. Sometimes there will also be a marginal note about an anecdote or other type of illustration. The alternative, the script, enables the speaker to try out the exact wording, phrases and pauses to achieve the greatest effect. The script will benefit from some marking or arrangement that will help you to find your place again as your eyes constantly flick from the page to the audience and back again. This can be underlining or using a highlighter. When using a script it is important not to make the reading too obvious. Head down, with no eye contact and little light and shade is a certain way of turning off the attention of the audience. Public figures increasingly use electronic prompters which project the script progressively through the presentation on to a glass screen some way in front of the speaker. By this means the script can be spoken with little break in eye contact with the audience. This will be too ambitious for most people, but the important thing is that the words should be *spoken* rather than *read*.

There are many variations of these basic methods of organizing the material, so that one approach is to use varying line length, while another is to use rows of dots to indicate pause or emphasis. Some people like to have their notes on small cards, so that they are unobtrusive, but this is difficult if the notes are more than headlines. Standard A4 paper should present no problem, if the notes are not stapled, are well laid out and can be handled discreetly. Never forget to number the pages or cards, as the next time you speak they may slip off your lap moments before you are due to begin, and they do not land on the floor in the same order that they were on your lap.

Most presentations benefit from using visual aids. You may use a model, a sample or even a person ('Here is our trainee of the month'), but mostly you will use visual images. Blackboards still exist and whiteboards are fairly common. The most rapidly growing type of visual image in presentation is that from a computer, projected on a screen, usually using a PowerPoint package. PowerPoint is so good that it can be dangerous. One problem is its relative sophistication technically. It has to be operated by someone who knows what he or she is doing and has confidence in being able to manage the computer rather than being managed by it. Every reader will have had experience of a presenter being baffled by a technical glitch that held up the presentation and knocked the presenter's confidence sideways. If the computer is being managed by someone other than the presenter, there is the potential difficulty of presenter and operator not always being coordinated.

The rationale for visual aids is that we remember what we see for longer than we remember what we are told, and we can sometimes understand what we see better than we can understand what we hear. Too much displayed material can obscure rather than illuminate what is being said. Television news provides a good example of how much can be used. The dominant theme is always the talking head with frequently intercut pieces of film. Very seldom do words appear on the screen and then usually as extracts from a speech or report, where a short sentence or passage is regarded as being especially meaningful. The other situation in which words and numbers appear is when facts are needed to illustrate an idea, so that ideas such as football scores or a change in the value of the US dollar almost always have the figures shown on the screen to clarify and illustrate. Seldom, however, will more than two or three numbers be displayed at the same time. Speakers need to remember the size of what they are displaying as well as its complexity. Material has to be big enough for people to read and simple enough for them to follow. Material also has to be timed to coincide with what is being said.

PowerPoint is a seductive toy. The box of tricks is enormous and too many people give a show, with clever figures dancing across the screen and other distractions. We must always remember what the purpose of the presentation is; clever or spectacular forms of display can become what people remember rather than the message that is to be conveyed. Television news is again an illustration. Between programmes there may be all manner of clever visual entertainment in brief clips. Once the news report begins there are no such fancy tricks.

KEY CONCEPT 36

The objective of your presentation is not for you to say what you have to say, but to ensure that the listeners depart with the appropriate understanding.

Chapter Sixteen
How to write a report

KEY CONCEPT 36 (AGAIN)

The objective of your presentation is not for you to say what you have to say, but to ensure that the listeners depart with the appropriate understanding.

The same principle applies if you have to write a report. Start by thinking of who will read it and what they will do with it. Who will read it determines how it is written. You cannot assume that they are familiar with the particular technical jargon and acronyms that you might be using, but neither can you assume that they are totally ignorant and patronize them with phrases such as '… for those unfamiliar with the first law of thermodynamics I should perhaps explain…'. What the reader will do with your report also determines how you write it, because you want them to do the right thing with it, or at least make a choice between alternatives. Action by the reader is the constant objective of the writer. If it is appropriate for you to make a recommendation, make sure that your recommended course of action flows logically from your preceding material. If you feel it is not appropriate to make a particular recommendation, you still write it in the same way, leading the reader to make the decision you think best. Reports should always be as brief as possible, but possible courses of action have to be fully justifiable from the material you have presented.

To make the report readable, you may use *appendices* to contain detailed data which illustrate points made in the report, but are not essential to understanding. Reference to an appendix may help to convince a reader of an argument that is presented in the report with enough evidence to convince most, but not enough to persuade the sceptical.

You may need a note of *sources*, if some readers want to refer to published material on which you have relied. You may not need full bibliographic details, but always sufficient to locate the material you have used.

Many reports have an *executive summary* that goes at the front. Most readers do not really want to read your report at all; they want a quick summary of the main points. This may annoy you, having spent hours perfecting your arguments and analysing your data, but the executive summary may lead the reader to refer to your main report for further explanation of recommendations or for the justification of a puzzling conclusion. It is, of course, a summary of the report that you have already written, not the other way round. You do not write some brief notes in summary and then expand them with more information for the full report. The summary requires thorough analysis and succinct explanation, with clear references, including page numbers, to the relevant sections of the full report.

Before the writing begins you need to *assemble and organize your material*. Chucking a pile of papers on the back seat of your car may be a form of assembling, but certainly not organizing. A simple method is to divide the pile into several piles of different categories, such as raw data, interview responses, external comparisons, suggestions, implications and probably not needed. Leaving out the 'probably not needed' for the time being, the next stage is to review the content of each pile, for three reasons. First, to recall everything and see where you want to go. Second, you may add some more of the material to that which is probably not needed. Third, as you begin to see where you want to go, you see what material you need to add: checks on the internet, visits to the library, telephone calls, finding and marking pages you may need to refer to in that book on the shelf behind you. If you now have a clear idea of what you want to achieve, and can see the logical way of getting there, you proceed to the next stage.

You now need a *framework*, to give a logical sequence to the writing and avoid risks of duplication, as well as presenting material early in the report that will be needed to justify points made later. Ways of doing this vary. One popular writer of fiction, Harold Robbins, worked with just a diagram above his typewriter showing how each of his characters was connected. An equally popular writer of much better fiction, John Grisham, works out a comprehensive and detailed structure for each book before he starts writing, so you have to employ the method that works for you. The framework comes from analysing the message that is to be sent in terms of the action expected and then subdividing the components of that message to be logically grouped. The framework may be modified during the writing until you are convinced that it is satisfactory.

As you are not writing popular fiction you are likely to need a structure that has the following features:

terms of reference;

who commissioned the report;

who has written it;

sources/methods used;

a list of acronyms;

executive summary at front (as well as normal summary at end);

contents list;

recommendations;

date.

This may not be the order in which they should appear, as you will want to draw the reader into the body of the report as soon as possible.

The logical groups will be in *sections*, each dealing with a distinct aspect of the report material. This emphasizes the logic of the way the material is grouped, but it is a part also of the communication to the reader, because the sections have titles, like headlines in a newspaper, summing up what the section contains. Titles should not tease or muddle the reader. 'Which way now?', for example, is an unhelpful title as it poses a question without giving any clue to the answer.

The *paragraph* is a unit of thought in the writing, dealing with a single topic or idea, and good paragraphing will ensure the material is read. Paragraphing also reassures the reader that there will be breathing spaces from time to time rather than a long, solid block of text to be ploughed through.

The appropriate length of paragraph varies with the material being written. Textbooks usually average 100–200 words, popular novels 60–75 and popular newspapers 30–40. Short paragraphs are easier for the reader, but reports will sometimes require detailed argument involving greater length. It is wise to keep the average under 120, if possible.

The *sentence* is the bit of writing between full stops, which makes sense and usually has a subject and a finite verb. The main difficulty in writing sentences is either that they are too long or that they set up expectations that are not realized. Writing sentences that are too long comes through adding on extra clauses and qualifications. Setting up expectations that are not realized comes from implying what is to come in the sentence, but then changing tack or emphasis without returning to the original thought.

Punctuation is important in making your meaning clear. Journalist Lynne Truss demonstrated this with a best-selling book in 2004 entitled *Eats Shoots and Leaves*. Written like that, the title accurately describes the eating habits of a giant panda.

Inserting a single comma changes it to describe a gangster eating dinner in a restaurant, executing a gangland rival at a nearby table and leaving before the police arrive. There are great subtleties of punctuation that can be deployed by pedants, but the basics are simple.

Punctuation

Comma makes a logical division within a sentence:

a To separate the subject from descriptive words or phrases: 'Charles, Prince of Wales, plays polo'.

b To separate clauses: 'If he scores, the crowd will cheer'.

c To separate items on a list: 'Her parents, husband and children came to watch'.

Semicolon links two sentences so closely related that a full stop would make too great a break: 'He didn't score; Jones did.'

Colon separates an announcement from what is announced: 'the order of play is as follows:'.

Apostrophe indicates either a possessive, 'the team's performance ...' or a missing syllable in abbreviations, 'it's time for tea'. There is so much uncertainty about the apostrophe that one often sees the quite unnecessary and misleading use in a simple plural. On the side of a delivery van, 'Laptops and PC's'; in a newspaper, 'The 1960's were the best time ever for popular music'.

Inverted commas can be quite confusing. Basically they are to identify in a sentence something that is being quoted, as in the above examples. A poor use that is sometimes found is to highlight when you are using a phrase which you know is not quite right, but you are too idle to express it properly: the fans are 'not best pleased' with the manager's performance.

Emphasis can be used in various ways, *italics*, <u>underlining</u>, emboldening, CAPITAL LETTERS or !!!!!!!! The important thing is to use them consistently and sparingly. This is quite different from using them as headings, marking stages in the development of your argument and signalling what is coming next. Here they are given different weight, with emboldened capitals being for the biggest sections, followed perhaps by italics for sections within a bigger section and so on. For simple emphasis the best method is in the choice of words. In popular media there is a tendency to rely on extravagant language; in a reality TV programme a singer is described by successive judges as 'fantastic', 'absolutely fantastic' and 'truly amazing'. Much more effective are words and phrases which provide emphasis by describing what has happened in a way that has meaning rather than simple euphoria.

A checklist for report writers

1 Before writing

   a What action do you expect from this report?

   b Who will read it?

   c How short can it be?

2 Framework

   a What precisely is the topic of the report?

   b How many components are there?

   c How can those best be grouped?

   d How are the components brought into sections?

   e Do the titles inform the reader?

   f Will the report, as outlined, produce the action specified in **1a**?

3 Writing the report

   a Is the average paragraph length less than 100 words?

   b Have you used more words than are needed?

c Have you used words that are precise and concrete rather than words that are vague and abstract?

d Have you any superfluous adverbs, adjectives and roundabout phrases?

e Have you shown the source of any facts quoted?

f Are any of the sentences too long?

4 Revising the report

    a Will the report as written produce the action specified in **1a**?

    b Is anything missing?

    c Are any calculations accurate?

    d Are the recommendations clear and justified?

    e Is the choice between alternatives clear?

    f Is any part of the report likely to cause offence to anyone? If so, can that be avoided?

    g What objections do you expect to the recommendations, and how will you deal with them?

    h Can any of the possible objections be prevented by rewriting part of the report?

5 Final presentation

    a Is the typing perfect and without spelling mistakes?

    b Are all the pages numbered?

    c Are abbreviations and symbols used consistently throughout?

    d Does the general appearance of the report encourage the reader to read it?

    e Is there a single-page summary of proposals?

    f Is the report being distributed to all the appropriate people?

    g If the report is confidential, is that indicated on the report and ensured by the method of distribution?

FURTHER READING

One classic work has been revised several times, the latest edition being published in 2000. It is only 95 pages, but an admirable guide: Strunk, WJ Jr and White, EB (2000) *The Elements of Style,* 4th edn, Longman, New York.

Chapter Seventeen
How to conduct a disciplinary interview

The least popular of all management activities is talking to people when things have gone wrong. Reading most books on management, you might think that things never go wrong. The writing has such an upbeat tone that it is *entirely* positive, enthusiastic, visionary, forward-looking and all the other qualities that are so important. Sometimes, however, things really do go wrong and have to be sorted out. The sorting out involves at some point a meeting between a dissatisfied manager and an employee who is seen as the cause of that dissatisfaction. Procedures, as required by law, can do no more than force meetings to take place: it is the meetings themselves that produce answers.

In Chapter 8 I argued that we should not approach these issues as a need for punishment, although that is a possible outcome. The approach in the following pages is based on the more accurate notion of discipline as attempting to modify the working behaviour of a subordinate, with the modification not necessarily involving punishment. It is to formulate an approach to the interview that aims for an adjustment in attitude, leading to changed behaviour. The manager believes that the employee's subsequent working behaviour will be satisfactory, the conflict of interest between the parties is resolved and the interview only succeeds when the behaviour change is confirmed in the manager's experience.

KEY CONCEPT 37

The disciplinary interview is to find ways of preventing a recurrence of unsatisfactory employee behaviour, not necessarily to rebuke or dismiss.

The nature of disciplinary interviewing

Discipline problems will have underlying reasons for the unsatisfactory behaviour, which need to be discovered before solutions to the problems can be attempted. The following sequence for the interview is suggested.

Preparation

First, check the procedural position to ensure that the impending interview is appropriate. In disciplinary matters, care is needed about the procedural step you are about to take, as the likelihood of penalties may already have been set up by warnings, thus reducing the scope for doing anything else in the impending interview apart from imposing a further penalty. The best interviews are where the manager pre-empts procedure, so the parties to the interview are less constrained by procedural rules. The manager will be at pains to explain that the interview is informal and without procedural implications.

What are the facts that you need to know? You need to collect evidence and consider how it may have been interpreted by intermediaries. This will include some basic details about the interviewee, but mainly it will be information about the aspects of the working performance that are unsatisfactory, and why. This often exists only in opinions that have been offered and prejudices that are held. This provides a poor basis for the start of a constructive interview, so you need to ferret out details, with as much factual corroboration as possible.

It is almost inevitable that the interviewee will start the interview defensively, expecting to be blamed for something and therefore ready to refute any allegations, probably deflecting blame elsewhere. The manager needs to anticipate the respondent's initial reaction and be prepared to deal with the reaction as well as with facts that have been collected. Unless the interview is at a very early, informal stage, the manager also needs to know about earlier warnings, cautions or penalties that have been invoked. More general information will also be required – not just the facts of the particular disciplinary situation, but a general understanding of the working arrangements and relationships. Also relevant may be the employee's length of service, type of training, previous experience and so forth.

Most managers will benefit from advice before starting. It is particularly important for anyone who is in the procedure to check the position with someone such as an HR manager, as management ability to sustain any action will largely depend on maintaining consistency with what the management has done with other employees previously. The manager may also have certain ideas of what could be done in terms of retraining, transfer or assistance with a domestic problem. The feasibility of such actions needs to be verified before broaching them with an employee whose work is not satisfactory.

The interview itself

Discipline starts from management dissatisfaction, so the opening move is for you to explain why it exists, dealing with the *facts* of the situation rather than managerial feelings of annoyance about them. This shows that you see the interview as a way of dealing with a problem of the working situation and not (at least not yet) as a way of dealing with an unsatisfactory employee.

If a staff member has been persistently late for a week, it would be unwise for a manager to open by saying, 'Your lateness this week has been deplorable', as the reason might turn out to be that the employee has a seriously ill child needing constant attendance through the night. Then you would be embarrassed and the potential for a constructive settlement of the matter would be jeopardized. An opening factual statement of the problem, 'You have been at least 20 minutes late each day this week ...', does not prejudge the reasons and is reasonably precise about the scale of the problem.

Now you need to know the explanation and ask the employee to say what the reasons for the problem are, perhaps also asking for comments on the seriousness of the problem itself, which the employee may regard as trivial but the manager regards as serious. Any such difference needs to be drawn out. Getting the employee's reaction is usually straightforward, but be prepared for one of two other types of reaction. Either you may need to probe because the employee is reluctant to open up, or there may be angry defiance. Disciplinary situations are at least disconcerting for employees and frequently very worrying, surrounded by feelings of hostility and mistrust, so that it is to be expected that some ill feeling will be pent up and waiting for the opportunity to be vented.

First possible move to closure: problem solving

If the employee sees something of the management view of the problem and if the manager understands the reasons for the problem, the next step is to seek a solution. A disciplinary problem is as likely to be solved by management action as by employee action. If the problem is lateness, one solution would be for the employee to catch an earlier bus, but another might be for the management to alter the working shift to which the employee is assigned. If the employee is disobeying orders, one solution would be for them to start obeying them, but another might be for the employee to be moved to a different job where orders are received from someone else. Some managers regard such thinking as unreasonable, on the grounds that the contract of employment places obligations on individual employees that they should meet despite personal inconvenience. However, the point is not how people *should* behave, but how they do. Can the contract of employment be enforced on an unwilling employee? Not if one is seeking such attitudes as enthusiasm and cooperation, or behaviour such as diligence and carefulness. The disenchanted employee can always meet the bare letter rather than the spirit of the contract.

The most realistic view is that many disciplinary problems require some action from both parties, some require action by the employee only and a small proportion requires management action only. The problem-solving session may quickly produce the possibility for further action and open up the possibility of closing the interview.

This simple, logical approach outlined so far may not be enough, owing to the unwillingness of employees to respond to disciplinary expectations. They may not want to be punctual or to do as they are instructed, or whatever the particular problem is. There is now a test of the power behind management authority. Three further steps can be taken, one after the other, although there will be occasions when it is necessary to move directly to the third.

Second possible move to closure: persuasion

The next move is to demonstrate to employees that they will not achieve what they want, if their behaviour does not change:

'You won't keep your earnings up if you don't meet targets.'
'It will be difficult to get your appointment confirmed when the probationary period is over if...'

By such means employees may see the advantages of changing their attitude and behaviour. If they are convinced, there is a strong incentive for them to alter, because they believe it to be in their own interests.

Third possible move to closure: disapproval

If you are still not getting anywhere, your next strategy is to suggest that continuing the behaviour will not please those whose goodwill the employee wishes to keep:

> 'The Management Development Panel are rather disappointed...'
> 'Some of the other people in the department feel that you are not pulling your weight.'

If using this method, be sure that what you say is both true and relevant. If you feel this is shirking the issue, use a version of 'I think this is just not good enough and expect you to do better'.

I asked for a restraint from judgement in the early stages of the interview, until the nature of the problem is clear. The time for judgement has now come, with the proper deployment of the rebuke or the caution.

Final possible move to closure: penalties

When all else fails or is clearly inappropriate, as with serious offences about which there is no doubt, penalties have to be invoked. In rare circumstances there may be the possibility of a fine, but usually the first penalty will be a formal warning as a preliminary to possible dismissal. In situations that are sufficiently grave, summary dismissal is both appropriate and possible within the legal framework.

Closure

You now need to think of the working situation that will follow. In closing the interview, aim for the flavour of closure to be as positive as possible so that all concerned put the disciplinary problem behind them. Where the outcome of the interview is to impose or confirm a dismissal, you will be concerned with the fairness and accuracy with which it is done, so that the possibility of tribunal hearings is reduced, if not prevented. It can never be appropriate to close an interview leaving the employee humbled and demoralized.

Chapter Eighteen
How to conduct a selection interview

Chapter 7 has already introduced the selection process and includes material on the interview, so this chapter is very short, little more than a checklist. You may like to re-read the earlier chapter, or at least Key Concepts 22–25, especially 25.

KEY CONCEPT 25 (AGAIN)

The selection interview should be an exchange of information, not a battle of wits.

Let's assume you are a single interviewer, aiming for an interview that is reasonably relaxed, working to a timetable that you will stick to closely.

Preparation

Review the job description, candidate specification and application forms or CVs. Note key issues and check points. Check timetable and interview setting. You now have in your mind, and in your notes, what the job is, what sort of skills and experience you need to look for, and you also have a preliminary idea of how the candidates match requirements.

The interview itself

Rapport

Begin with a welcome that is friendly and explains briefly who you are. Continue with rapport, to set up the exchange through brief inconsequential discussion. Explain procedure, maintaining a relaxed, friendly manner.

Exchange

You now move to the substance of the interview as you ask questions and the candidate answers, but it is still an exchange rather than an inquiry as you are giving information by the content of your questions and some of the replies will be preceded by queries for clarification and information, but you must keep hold of the exchange so that it follows your strategy to discover whether this person is right for this job without it becoming a pleasant rambling chat. The most productive questions invite the candidate to talk, such as 'Could you give me an outline of your present duties?', but you will also need closed questions to check on matters of fact or to clarify inconsistencies, such as 'When did you leave Amalgamated Widgets?' Never use leading questions which imply the answer you want, such as 'Would you agree with me that...?'

Exchange needs a logical sequence, such as working chronologically through the application form, which the candidate can understand and keeps your growing understanding in order.

As well as asking questions you listen, observe and take notes. The notes are to assist your recollection subsequently and may well be scribbled on the application form adjacent to what the candidate has written, so that the notes can be briefer.

Remember your key issues and check points.

After the interview

Consider the person/job match by reviewing the job information in the job description and the candidate specification and by reviewing the candidate information in the application form, your interview notes, test scores (if any) and references (if any).

Decide whether there is a good match or not, and the significance of any poor fitting. Consult with team members and decide (a) to whom the job offer should be made, with possible alternatives, and (b) the terms of the offer.

After a job offer has been accepted, notify the unsuccessful candidates.

Chapter Nineteen
How to do performance appraisal

Appraising performance is not precise measurement but subjective assessment. It is frequently done badly with quite serious results, but when it is done well it can be invaluable for the business, and literally life transforming for the appraisee. After the disciplinary interview it is probably the most dreaded interview for both appraisers and appraisees.

The appraisal interview style

The different styles of appraisal interview were succinctly described 50 years ago as being either *problem solving, tell-and-sell* or *tell-and-listen*. This remains the most widely adopted means of identifying the way to tackle the interview.

The *problem-solving* style is where the appraiser encourages the appraisee to start reviewing the performance, identifying any problems and how they could be overcome. This means that the appraisee is determining how the interview is going to start, with fuller evaluation emerging from discussion with the appraiser. At least initially, the problems are those that the appraisee recognizes and is able to acknowledge; this is a vital step towards the problems being solved. This is certainly a most effective style provided that both the appraiser and appraisee have the skill and ability to handle it. The upcoming suggestions are based on this style, but it is not the only style.

In *tell-and-sell*, the appraiser acts as judge, using the interview to tell the appraisee the result of the appraisal and how to improve. This 'ski instructor' approach can be appropriate when the appraisees have little experience and have not developed enough self-confidence to analyse their own performance.

Tell-and-listen still casts the appraiser in the role of judge, passing on the outcome of an appraisal that has already been completed and listening to reactions. Both of these approaches could sometimes change the assessment, as well as enabling the two people to have a reasonably frank exchange. They can be appropriate where the appraisee is relatively inexperienced and cannot therefore set the agenda effectively.

The problem-solving approach appears to be the most civilized and searching, but not all appraisal situations call for this style, not all appraisees are ready for it and not all appraisers normally behave in this way.

The appraisal interview sequence

Certain aspects of the appraisal interview are the same as those of the selection interview as described in the last chapter. The appraiser determines the framework of the interview, there is the same need to open in a way that develops mutual confidence as far as possible and there is the use of closed and open-ended questions, reflection and summarizing. It is also a difficult meeting for the two parties. The appraiser has to have a degree of confidence and personal authority in their relationship with the appraisee. For the appraisee there are concerns about career progress, job security, the ongoing working relationship with the appraiser and basic anxieties relating to self-esteem and dealing with criticism.

The main difference between selection and appraisal is that the objective is to reach an understanding that will have some impact on the future performance of the appraisee; it is not simply to formulate a judgement by collecting information, as in selection. To use a medical metaphor, a surgeon carrying out hip replacements will select patients for surgery on the basis of inquiring about their symptoms and careful consideration of the evidence. The surgeon asks the questions, makes the decision and implements it. A physician examining a patient who is overweight and short of breath may rapidly make the decision that the patient needs to lose weight and take more exercise. It is, however, not the physician but the patient who has to implement that decision. The physician can help with diet sheets, regular check-ups and terrifying advice; the real challenge is how to get the patient to respond. The easy part of appraisal is sorting out the facts. The difficult bit is actually bringing about a change in performance. The interview, like the discussion in the physician's consulting rooms, is crucial in bringing about a change of attitude, fresh understanding and commitment to action.

Preparation

The appraiser should brief the appraisee on the form of the interview, possibly asking for a self-appraisal form to be completed in advance. This will only be appropriate if the scheme requires it. As we have seen, self-appraisal gives the appraisee some initiative, ensures that the discussion will be about matters which the appraisee can handle and about 'real stuff'.

The appraiser has to review all the available evidence on the appraisee's performance, including reports, records or other material regarding the period under review. Most important will be the previous appraisal and its outcomes.

Most of the points made about preparing for the selection interview apply to appraisal as well, especially the setting. Taking time and trouble to ensure that the setting and supportive nature of the discussion take account of the appraisee's needs really pays off in getting a positive response.

Interview structure

A recommended structure for a performance appraisal interview is given in Table 19.1.

TABLE 19.1   A recommended structure for a performance appraisal interview

Purpose and rapport	Agree the purpose and structure for the meeting.
Factual review	Appraiser reviews known facts about performance in previous period. Appraisee agrees or queries for clarification.
Appraisee views	Appraisee asked to comment on period under review. What has gone well and what less well; what could be improved; what was liked and what disliked; possible new objectives.
Appraiser views	Appraiser adds own perspective, asks questions and disagrees, as appropriate, with what appraisee has said.
Problem solving	Discussion of any differences and how they can be resolved.
Objective setting	Agreeing on what action should be taken, and by whom, with targets and review dates.

Rapport is unusual because it attempts to smooth the interaction between two people who probably have an easy social relationship, but now find themselves ill at ease. This is not the sort of conversation they are used to having together, so they have to find new ground-rules. The appraisal interview itself may be easier to introduce and handle if, as generally recommended, there are mini-reviews throughout the year. This should ensure that there are no surprises, and the two people concerned get used to having performance-focused meetings, however informal. The opening of the interview itself still needs care. The mood needs to be light, but not trivial, as the appraisee has to be encouraged towards candour rather than gamesmanship.

Factual review is reviewing aspects of the previous year's work that are unproblematic. The appraiser should begin by reviewing the main facts about the performance, not expressing opinions about them but merely summarizing as a mutual reminder, perhaps reviewing previous objectives set and the outcome of the previous appraisal. This will be key in any later discussion by confirming such matters as length of time in the job, any personnel changes in the period, turnover figures, training undertaken and so forth. The appraiser does most, but not all, of the talking, and can isolate those aspects of performance that are clearly satisfactory, mention them and comment favourably. This sustains rapport and provides the basic reassurance the appraisee needs in order to avoid being defensive. The favourable aspects of performance will to some extent be *discovered* by the factual review process. It is important that 'the facts speak for themselves' rather than appraiser judgement being offered, for example:

> Those figures look very good. How do they compare with...?
> That's X per cent up on the quarter and Y per cent on the
> year... That's one of the best results in the group. You must
> be pleased with that ... How on earth did you do it?

The evidence, including that collected throughout the year as we suggested earlier, is there before the eyes of both parties, with the appraiser pointing out and emphasizing. It is also specific rather than general, precise rather than vague. This type of approach invariably raises the question from appraisers about what to do in a situation of poor performance. Appraising stars is easy; what about the duds? The answer is that all appraisees have some aspects of their performance on which favourable comment can be made, and the appraisal process actually identifies strengths that might have been previously obscured by the general impression of someone who is not very good. The appraiser may discover something on which to build, having previously thought the case was hopeless. If there is not some feature of the performance that can be isolated in this way, the appraiser probably has a management or disciplinary problem that should have been tackled earlier.

Appraisee views on things that are not as good as they might be in performance, areas of possible improvement and how these might be addressed will only be offered by the appraisee if there has been effective positive reinforcement in the previous stages of the interview. People can only acknowledge shortcomings about performance when they are reasonably sure of their ground. Now the appraisee is examining areas of dissatisfaction by the process of discussing them with the appraiser, with whom it is worth having the discussion, because of the appraiser's expertise, information and 'helicopter view'. The likely result of debating these matters is either that they will be shown to be less worrying than they seemed when viewed only from the single perspective of the appraisee, and ways of dealing with them become apparent, or that they are confirmed as matters needing attention.

This stage in the interview is fraught with difficulties for the manager, and is one of the reasons why an alternative style is sometimes preferred. Some appraisees do not want to discuss, but to be told by the manager, whose job it is. In this situation tell-and-sell or tell-and-listen are more appropriate.

Appraiser views can now be added to the list of areas for improvement. In many instances there will be no additions to make, but usually there are some needs that the appraisee cannot, or will not, see. If they are put at this point in the interview, there is the best chance that they will be understood, accepted and acted upon. It is not possible to guarantee success. Demoralized collapse or bitter resentment is always a possibility, but this is the time to try, as the appraisee has developed a basis of reassurance and has come to terms with some shortcomings that he or she had already recognized.

The appraiser has to judge whether any further issues can be raised and if so, how many. This feedback needs care and thought because it is precisely what it describes. As in telecommunications, which was mentioned in Chapter 6, the strength and quality of the message from the sender are improved by positive feedback from the receiver. In appraisal, views on performance from the appraisee provide the basis on which the appraiser views have to be built, because what the appraisee has said and acknowledged is what the appraisee can 'live with'. That self-awareness now needs to be enlarged in a way that the appraisee can continue to understand and acknowledge. Some of the problems already acknowledged will be dealt with simply by the appraiser putting them in a different light; others will be dealt with by an offer of specific help; some may need to be added. None of us can cope with confronting all our shortcomings, all at the same time, and the appraiser's underlying management responsibility is to ensure that the appraisee is not made less competent by the appraisal interview. Appraisers do not use the interview to justify their criticisms; they use it to enhance the appraisee's performance.

Problem solving is the process of talking out the areas for improvement that have been identified, so that the appraisee can cope with them. Underlying causes are uncovered through further discussion. Gradually huge problems come into clearer and less forbidding perspective, perhaps through being analysed and broken up into different components. Possibilities for action, by both appraiser and appraisee, become clear.

These central stages of the interview, factual exchange, appraisee views, appraiser views and problem solving, need to move in that sequence. Some may be brief, but none should be omitted and the sequence should not alter.

The final stage of objective setting is to agree what is to be done. Actions need to be agreed and nailed down, so that they actually take place. One of the biggest causes of appraisal failure is with action not being taken, so the objectives set must be not only mutually acceptable, but also deliverable. It is likely that some action will be needed from the appraiser as well as some from the appraisee.

Making appraisal work

The criteria for appraisal must be genuinely related to success or failure in the job, rather than vaguely defined personal qualities. They should also be amenable to objective, rather than subjective, judgement and they should appear fair and relevant to the appraisee. An excellent performance appraisal system (oh yes, some are!) is of no use at all if managers do not know how to use the system to best effect. Appraisal interviews need to be supported by follow-up action. Work plans agreed by appraiser and appraisee need to be monitored to ensure that they actually take place, or that they are modified in accordance with changed circumstances or priorities. Training needs should be identified and plans made to meet them.

KEY CONCEPT 38

Performance appraisal is often done badly; it has considerable potential, when done well.

Appendix
Key concepts

KEY CONCEPT 1

Managing with people is working with *people as well as being in charge. We all have to build effective relationships with colleagues in order to get the most out of our jobs while producing good results. Also, we all have to understand how our particular organization works and how we can use it to produce good results. Personnel or human resource management is different. It is a specialist role in a business to enable everyone else in the business to be good at managing with people.*

KEY CONCEPT 2

People will support and make a success of what they have helped to create.

KEY CONCEPT 3

Managers need to retain their specialist skills if they are to keep the respect of those with whom they work at all levels.

KEY CONCEPT 4

Managers have two core tasks: working out agendas for action (what to do) and developing networks of contacts to facilitate implementing those agendas (how to get it done).

KEY CONCEPT 5

Typically managers spend well over half of their working day in conversation and constantly switching between topics.

KEY CONCEPT 6

The central elements of the work that managers do can be classified as specialist, administrative or managerial. The balance between these three varies between different jobs and even between people with jobs that are notionally identical. Each manager needs to consider very carefully the balance between the three that will lead to effective performance and job satisfaction.

KEY CONCEPT 7

The manager is not alone. Everybody at work has some degree of independence, but they are inescapably part of something. You are actually part of several things which provide a framework for what you do but also provide a limit to what you can do. You are not alone.

KEY CONCEPT 8

Your job title tells people what you are; this is important. The title of the job you are doing gives you a recognized place and function in the various contexts and networks within which you work. This is a necessary prerequisite to effective working with clients and colleagues.

KEY CONCEPT 9

Managers are both enabled and restricted by their contexts: job title, economic, political, social, international.

KEY CONCEPT 10

Strategy describes the sense of purpose and overall direction of the business. It is developed with varying degrees of formality according to the size, complexity and ownership of the organization. It is forward-looking and must be realistic as well as motivating the necessary actions to realize the objectives.

KEY CONCEPT 11

Policy complements strategy. Strategic thinking needs policies to make it happen and policies are also needed to ensure the business is conducted in a way that fits the organization within its evolving economic, political and social contexts.

KEY CONCEPT 12

Procedures enable the right future to happen. They provide recipes for people to follow; they ensure consistency in the way things are done; they give autonomy to individuals; and they are a means of management control.

KEY CONCEPT 13

Though essential, procedures can cause problems.

KEY CONCEPT 14

Too often targets generate the wrong behaviour. Either the targets become misaligned with the behaviour needed in a changing situation, or the behaviour is too narrowly focused on the target at the expense of the wholeness of the job to be done.

KEY CONCEPT 15

Hierarchy works because: (a) a system of roles and jobs is more predictable than a gathering of people; (b) it distributes and rations necessary power; (c) it controls and limits conflict; (d) it works through differentiation and integration.

KEY CONCEPT 16

Three broad forms of structure are: (a) entrepreneurial to emphasize central power; (b) bureaucratic to distribute power in a complex business; (c) matrix to coordinate diverse expertise.

KEY CONCEPT 17

The organization of departments has two elements: (a) grouping people mainly according to complementary skills or organizational efficiency; (b) organizing people according to their activities, their jobs, the authority they need and the connections between them.

KEY CONCEPT 18

The culture of a business is shared values and behaviour. Employees need to understand the culture so that they can adapt to it. Managers need to work within the culture in order to produce effective working.

KEY CONCEPT 19

Culture is hard to change. Those creating a business may be able to build a corporate culture from scratch by personal example, explanation and exhortation. Those aiming to change an existing corporate culture will find it much harder and slower.

KEY CONCEPT 20

Communication between people always uses code. Codes can be misinterpreted.

KEY CONCEPT 21

The method of communication has to be selected according to the nature of the message and the recipients. Simply providing information is not sufficient; it has to be sent in a form that will elicit the desired response.

KEY CONCEPT 22

In selecting people for your team, make sure you pick the right people, not just those you like.

KEY CONCEPT 23

Selection matches the needs of the business with those of the recruit; many of these needs are the same.

KEY CONCEPT 24

The requirements of the job must be thoroughly clear before the type of candidate is specified.

KEY CONCEPT 25

The selection interview should be an exchange of information, not a battle of wits.

KEY CONCEPT 26

Grievance and discipline are ways of resolving difficulties in the employment relationship. They are not about punishment or grumbling.

KEY CONCEPT 27

People at work are predisposed to obey those in a role that gives them a defined authority.

KEY CONCEPT 28

A complaint is an opportunity for a manager to manage. A grievance is the outcome of a manager not being able to manage.

KEY CONCEPT 29

Teaching people requires an approach appropriate to what in the learner is to be developed: practical skill or drill, understanding something more complex, learning how to work with other people.

KEY CONCEPT 30

Coaching is a skill in managing a relationship with someone seeking to improve their working performance.

KEY CONCEPT 31

For effective performance to come from your people they need (a) to be the right people in the right job, (b) the right lines of communication, (c) planning, goals and standards, (d) guidance and support from you and (e) appraisal.

KEY CONCEPT 32

Managing the boss is an integral part of producing effective performance; people management is not all one way.

KEY CONCEPT 33

Methods of building your network include getting to know better those on whom you feel dependent, developing a reputation as a good team player (by deeds not words), practising working a room and using business cards.

KEY CONCEPT 34

A person chairing a meeting needs to answer these questions: (1) Is the purpose of this meeting to decide, to recommend or to share information? (2) What should the agenda be? (3) What can I expect to be achieved at this meeting? (4) How can I chair the meeting in a way that is most effective for the agenda and to achieve my objective?

KEY CONCEPT 35

Rank and file members of the meeting can make their best contributions by: (1) looking for solutions that others will support; (2) building on contributions from others that you regard as constructive; (3) monitoring the mood of the meeting to judge when best to make your contributions; (4) working through the chair.

KEY CONCEPT 36

The objective of your presentation is not for you to say what you have to say, but to ensure that the listeners depart with the appropriate understanding.

KEY CONCEPT 37

The disciplinary interview is to find ways of preventing a recurrence of unsatisfactory employee behaviour, not necessarily to rebuke or dismiss.

KEY CONCEPT 38

Performance appraisal is often done badly; it has considerable potential, when done well.

Index

(page numbers in *italic* indicate tables)

CPSIA information can be obtained at www.ICGtesting.com
Printed in the USA
BVOW030843200313

315802BV00006B/4/P

9 780749 466749